L&T Infotech

Placement Papers

Latest Edition

Practice Kit

10 Tests

10 Mock Test

Based On Real Exam Pattern

✓ Thoroughly Revised and Updated

✓ Detailed Analysis of all MCQs

Title : L&T Infotech Placement Papers
Author Name : Mr. Rohit Manglik
Published By : EduGorilla Community Pvt. Ltd.
Publishers Address : 12/651, First Floor Opp. Arvindo Park, Near Jama Masjid, Indira Nagar, Lucknow, Uttar Pradesh-226016, India

Copyright EduGorilla

ISBN : 978-93-55560-31-5
Second Edition

Disclaimer EduGorilla

Although the author and publisher have made every effort to ensure the accuracy of information in this book, we do not assume any responsibility to errors and hereby disclaim any liability to any party for any loss, damage, or disruption caused by errors or omissions, whether such errors or omissions result from negligence, accident, or any other cause.

Compiled and created by EduGorilla Community Pvt. Ltd

Printed By EduGorilla Community Pvt. Ltd.

ROHIT MANGLIK
CEO, EduGorilla

Editor's Note

Dear Applicants,

People say *"Success comes to those who work hard."* But I've seen people working hard for their exams day in and day out for marginal success. While others succeed in their examinations by putting in just half the work. So are they God Gifted? No! I believe that it's because they work *smart* and not just *hard*. Similarly, for your exams, you should strategize your preparation so as to increase the likelihood of success. Well with EduGorilla get ready to increase your *chances of selection* in your exam by *16x*.

EduGorilla helps you in not only working *hard* but also working in a *smart and strategic* manner. With EduGorilla's preparation package, you get a chance to make your exam preparation easy, and a fun learning path towards selection. Finding the right path to your preparations can be difficult if you don't know in which direction to head. Don't worry, we have you covered! EduGorilla will be your guide to success in your journey. With our Preparation Package, you can prepare strategically and beat the exam in just one attempt.

EduGorilla's Preparation Package includes-

- **Test Series**
- **Books**

Our preparation package is handcrafted as per the latest changes, expert opinions, and students' discretion. Thus, enabling you to get through each stage of the selection process for your exam.

Our Books are designed by the teachers and experts of the respective exam with a combined 150+ years of experience; to provide you with easy, efficient, and effective learning. Our books are smart, in the sense that not only do they give you the answers to the questions but also provide similar questions for practice.

EduGorilla's competent Test Series gives you real-time experience and confidence through which you can clear your offline or online exam in just one attempt. We currently host 83,000+ mock tests for 1,440+ competitive and academic exams.

Thus, EduGorilla misses no chance to assist you in your preparation and covers all stages of the exam, so that you don't have to look anywhere else.

We provide complete preparation packages for defense, banking, teaching, and other National & State-Level exams. Hence, it doesn't matter which exam you aspire to because you will reach your success.

ALL THE BEST !

Let EduGorilla be your Guide to Success.

Rohit Manglik,
Founder and CEO, EduGorilla

INTRODUCTION

EduGorilla focuses on guiding students to succeed in their examinations. With that in mind, our book, titled "L&T Infotech : Placement Papers", has been drafted through the collective efforts of our distinguished experts with 150+ years of combined experience. This book consists of questions that are created following the latest changes in the syllabus and exam pattern. We compiled the book on the basis of questions that are most likely to appear in the L&T Infotech. Through EduGorilla's "L&T Infotech : Placement Papers" your chances of success will increase 16x.

EduGorilla does this through our Complete Preparation Package. This package consists of well-conceptualized and structured content in the form of questions that are tailor-made according to your needs and will help you practice for exams in a smart way by pinpointing all the necessary information. It also provides hints and solutions, along with a smart answer sheet for your self-evaluation. You can assess your shortcomings and work accordingly on areas that may require more of your attention.

EduGorilla promises to help you succeed in your examination and accomplish your dream goals. We believe in our aspirants and see them at the top of the merit list. And the first step towards the top is to start preparing with us. EduGorilla's "L&T Infotech : Placement Papers" includes the following attributes.

- Well-Researched Content
- Top-Notch Quality
- Detailed Answers and Analysis
- Smart Answer Sheet
- Exam Relevant Questions

Therefore, EduGorilla fortifies your preparation and makes it durable enough to help you stand tall and beat the examination.

L&T Infotech
Scan QR code for Eligibility, Exam Pattern, Syllabus and more.

Book ID: 0837

TABLE OF CONTENTS

Mock Test 01

Q.1 What will be the output of the following pseudo code for arr[]= 1,2,3,4,5

```
initialize i,n
intialize and array of size n
accept the values for the array
for o to n
arr[i] = arr[i]+arr[i+1]
end for
print the array elements
```

A. 3 5 7 9 5 **B.** 3 5 7 9 11
C. 3 5 9 15 20 **D.** Error

Q.2 Find the output of the following pseudo-code:

```
Integer x, y, z;
x=0
y = 1
x = y = z = 8
Print x
```

A. 0 **B.** 8
C. 1 **D.** None of the above

Q.3 What will be the output of the following pseudo code?

For input a = 5 & b = 5.

```
function (input a, input b)
If (a< b)
return function (b, a)
elseif (b != 0)
return (a * function (a, b - 1))
else
return 0
```

A. 15625 **B.** 625 **C.** 3125 **D.** 525

Q.4 What will be the output of the following pseudo code.

```
initialize char c
set c= a
print "%d",a
```

A. 64 **B.** 97 **C.** A **D.** Error

Q.5 What will be the output of the following code?

```
#include"stdio.h"
int main ()
{
char c,a,b;
c='f';
a='s';
b='x';
int sum= c+a+b;
printf ("%d", sum);
}
```

A. 324 **B.** 315 **C.** 320 **D.** 337

Q.6 What do we use to define a block of code in Python language?

A. Key **B.** Brackets
C. Indentation **D.** None of these

Q.7 Why does the name of local variables start with an underscore discouraged?

A. To identify the variable
B. It confuses the interpreter
C. It indicates a private variable of a class
D. None of these

Q.8 Study the following function:

round(4.576)

What will be the output of this function?

A. 4 **B.** 4576 **C.** 576 **D.** 5

Q.9 Which of the following modifiers can be used for a variable so that it can be accessed by any thread or a part of a program?

A. Global **B.** Transient
C. Volatile **D.** Default

Q.10 What will be the output of this code:

```
#include "stdio.h"
int main()
{
int x, y = 5, z = 5;
x = y == z;
printf("%d", x);
getchar();
return 0;
}
```

A. 0 **B.** 1
C. 5 **D.** Compiler Error

Q.11 What will be the output of this code:

```
#include"stdio.h"
int main()
{
int i = 1, 2, 3;
printf("%d", i);
return 0;
}
```

A. 1 **B.** 3
C. Garbage value **D.** Compile time error

Q.12 What will be the output of this code:

```
#include"stdio.h"
int main()
{
int i = (1, 2, 3);
printf("%d", i);
return 0;
}
```

A. 1 **B.** 3
C. Garbage value **D.** Compile time error

Q.13 What will be the output of this code:

```
#include<stdio.h>
int main()
{
int i;
i = 1, 2, 3;
printf("%d", i);
return 0;
}
```

A. 1 **B.** 3
C. Garbage value **D.** Compile time error

Q.14 Predict the output of following C++ program.

```
#include<iostream>
using namespace std;
class Test
{
static int x;
public:
Test() { x++; }
static int getX() {return x;}
};
int Test::x = 0;
int main()
{
cout<< Test::getX()<< " ";
Test t[5];
cout<< Test::getX();
}
```

A. 0 0 **B.** 5 5
C. 0 5 **D.** Compiler Error

Q.15 Predict the output of following C++ program.

```
#include<iostream>
using namespace std;
class Player
{
private:
int id;
static int next_id;
public:
int getID() { return id; }
Player() { id = next_id++; }
};
int Player::next_id = 1;
int main()
{
Player p1;
Player p2;
Player p3;
cout<< p1.getID()<< " ";
cout<< p2.getID()<< " ";
cout<< p3.getID();
return 0;
}
```

A. Compiler Error **B.** 1 2 3
C. 1 1 1 **D.** 3 3 3

Q.16 In how many ways can an object be passed to a function?

A. 1 **B.** 2 **C.** 3 **D.** 4

Q.17 If an object is passed by value, then__________.

A. A new copy of object is created implicitly
B. The object itself is used
C. Address of the object is passed
D. A new object is created with new random values

Q.18 Pass by address passes the address of object _______ and pass by reference passes the address of the object _______.

A. Explicitly, explicitly
B. Implicitly, implicitly
C. Explicitly, Implicitly
D. Implicitly, explicitly

Q.19 If an object is passed by reference, the changes made in the function _________.

A. Are reflected to the main object of caller function too.
B. Are reflected only in local scope of the called function.
C. Are reflected to the copy of the object that is made during pass.
D. Are reflected to caller function object and called function object also.

Q.20 Which of the following feature is also known as run-time binding or late binding?

A. Dynamic typing **B.** Dynamic loading
C. Dynamic binding **D.** Data hiding

Q.21 Which of the following terms is just the connection of networks that can be joined together?

A. Internet
B. Virtual private network
C. Intranet
D. Extranet

Q.22 A computer checks the ____ of user names and passwords for a match before granting access.

A. Website **B.** Network
C. Backup file **D.** Database

Q.23 Network components are connected to the same cable in the ____ topology.

A. Star **B.** Ring **C.** Bus **D.** Mesh

Q.24 Which statement describes a spanning-tree network that has converged?

A. All switch and bridge ports are in the forwarding state.
B. All switch and bridge ports are assigned as either root or designated ports.
C. All switch and bridge ports are in either the forwarding or blocking state.
D. All switch and bridge ports are either blocking or looping.

Q.25 WPA2 is used for security in ________.

A. Internet **B.** Bluetooth
C. Wi-Fi **D.** (A) and (B) both

Q.26 Which of the following is generally used for performing tasks like creating the structure of the relations, deleting relation?

A. DML(Data Manipulation Language)
B. Query
C. Relational Schema
D. DDL(Data Definition Language)

Q.27 Which of the following provides the ability to query information from the database and insert tuples into, delete tuples from, and modify tuples in the database?

A. DML (Data Manipulation Language)
B. DDL (Data Definition Language)
C. Query
D. Relational Schema

Q.28 A Database Management System is a type of ________ software.

A. System software
B. Application software
C. General software
D. Both (A) and (C)

Q.29 There are similarities between the instructor entity set and the secretary entity set in the sense that they have several attributes that are conceptually the same across the two entity sets: namely, the identifier, name, and salary attributes. This process is called-

A. Commonality **B.** Specialization
C. Generalization **D.** Similarity

Q.30 Functional dependencies are a generalization of-

A. Key dependencies
B. Relation dependencies
C. Database dependencies
D. External dependencies

Q.31 The given Query can also be replaced with______:

SELECT name, course_id
FROM instructor, teaches
WHERE instructor_ID= teaches_ID;

A. Select name,course_id from teaches,instructor where instructor_id=course_id;
B. Select name, course_id from instructor natural join teaches;
C. Select name, course_id from the instructor;
D. Select course_id from instructor join teaches;

Q.32 Which one of the following given statements possibly contains the error?

A. Select * from emp where empid = 10003;
B. Select empid from emp where empid = 10006;
C. Select empid from emp;
D. Select empid where empid = 1009 and Lastname = 'GELLER';

Q.33 Complete the following query-

SELECT emp_name
FROM department
WHERE dept_name LIKE ' ____ Computer Science';

In the above-given Query, which of the following can be placed in the Query's blank portion to select the "dept_name" that also contains Computer Science as its ending string?

A. & **B.** _ **C.** % **D.** $

Q.34 What type of commands are required to perform various tasks in DOS?

A. Internal commands **B.** External commands
C. Valuable commands **D.** Primary commands

Q.35 If you want to execute more than one program at a time, the systems software you are using must be capable of:

A. Word processing **B.** Virtual memory
C. Compiling **D.** Multitasking

Q.36 The ________ begins with a series of parameter entity definitions.

A. DTD **B.** SGML
C. XML **D.** None of these

Q.37 Which of the following tag is used to insert a line-break in HTML?

A.
 B. <a> **C.** <pre> **D.** <b>

Q.38 How to create an unordered list (a list with the list items in bullets) in HTML?

A. <ul> **B.** <ol> **C.** <li> **D.** <i>

Q.39 RAD stands for-

A. Rapid Application Development
B. Required Application Development
C. Rapid Application Developers
D. Rapid Application Disposition

Q.40 Which of the following are valid step in SDLC framework?

A. Requirement Gathering
B. System Analysis
C. Software Design
D. All of the above

// Smart Answer Sheet //

Correct Indicates percentage of students who answered questions correctly.

Skipped Indicates percentage of students who skipped questions.

Q.	Ans.	Correct	Skipped
1	A	26.47 %	9.47 %
2	B	46.45 %	15.71 %
3	C	24.21 %	13.26 %
4	B	26.89 %	17.98 %
5	D	17.6 %	15.9 %
6	C	39.49 %	14.85 %
7	C	33.62 %	15.77 %
8	D	36.37 %	15.04 %
9	C	20.54 %	15.46 %
10	B	20.23 %	15.77 %
11	D	27.14 %	13.45 %
12	B	22.25 %	15.22 %
13	D	23.29 %	9.9 %
14	C	24.21 %	16.32 %
15	B	32.15 %	15.04 %
16	C	29.03 %	13.21 %
17	A	27.2 %	15.71 %
18	C	35.88 %	16.56 %
19	A	34.54 %	6.47 %
20	C	51.47 %	12.65 %
21	A	39.18 %	12.65 %
22	D	48.17 %	16.56 %
23	C	42.48 %	5.87 %
24	C	27.51 %	16.74 %
25	C	43.28 %	16.13 %
26	D	24.57 %	16.81 %
27	A	47.92 %	9.11 %
28	A	24.14 %	16.69 %
29	C	34.35 %	12.9 %
30	A	21.15 %	15.4 %
31	B	32.7 %	15.53 %
32	D	31.97 %	13.45 %
33	C	30.07 %	9.48 %
34	B	28.36 %	16.81 %
35	D	47.98 %	13.94 %
36	A	25.24 %	14.55 %
37	A	49.57 %	17.48 %
38	A	43.4 %	16.5 %
39	A	40.22 %	17.36 %
40	D	43.03 %	17.42 %

Performance Analysis	
Avg. Score (%)	32.5%
Toppers Score (%)	100.0%
Your Score	

//Hints and Solutions//

1. The following pseudo-code will add the first element with the second, the second element with the third, the third element with the fourth and the fourth element with the fifth, the fifth element will remain as it is
and so, the output will be 3 5 7 9 5.

Hence, the correct option is (A).

2. In this question, the value of x is initialized as 0 and y as 1 in the beginning. Later the value 8 is assigned to the variable z and the value of z is assigned to the variable y and the value of y is assigned to the variable x. Finally, the value of x is updated as 8.

Hence, the correct option is (B).

3. Function $(5,5)$ will return $5 \times$ function $(5,4)$.

Function $(5,4)$ will return $5 \times 5 \times$ function $(5,3)$.

Function $(5,3)$ will return $5 \times 5 \times 5 \times$ function $(5,2)$.

Function $(5,2)$ will return $5 \times 5 \times 5 \times 5$ function $(5,1)$.

Function $(5,0)$ will return $5 \times 5 \times 5 \times 5 \times 5 = 3125$.

Hence, the correct option is (C).

4. The code will print the ASCII value of the entered character. The full form of ASCII is the American Standard Code for information interchange. It is a character encoding scheme used for electronics communication. Each character or a special character is represented by some ASCII code, and each ascii code occupies 7 bits in memory. The numerical value, or order, of an ASCII character. There are 128 standard ASCII characters, numbered from 0 to 127.

Hence, the correct option is (B).

5. The following code will add the ASCII values of the given characters
f = 102
s = 115
x = 120
sum = 102+115+120 = 337

Hence, the correct option is (D).

6. Python uses indentation to define blocks of code. Indentations are simply spaces or tabs used as an indicator that is part of the indent code child. A code block (body of a function, loop, etc.) starts with indentation and ends with the first unindented line. The amount of indentation is up to you, but it must be consistent throughout that block. As used in curly braces C, C++, and Java.

Hence, the correct option is (C).

7. Since there is no concept of private variables in Python language, the major underscore is used to denote variables that cannot be accessed from outside the class. local variable names beginning with an underscore discouraged because they are used to indicate a private variables of a class.

Hence, the correct option is (C).

8. The round function is a built-in function in the Python language that round-off the value (like 3.85 is 4), so the output of this function will be 5.

Hence, the correct option is (D).

9. In Java, we can modify the values of a variable with the help of a reserved keyword known as volatile. It is a different way of making a class thread-safe. Thread-safe means that the methods and objects of a class are accessible by multiple threads at the same time.

The volatile keyword is not a replacement of a synchronized block or method as it does not remove the need for synchronization among the atomic actions.

Global is not a reserved keyword in Java. The transient and default are keywords in Java, but they are not used for accessing a variable by a thread from any part of the program.

Hence, the correct option is (C).

10. The crux of the question lies in the statement x = y==z. The operator == is executed before = because precedence of comparison operators (<=, >= and ==) is higher than assignment operator =. The result of a comparison operator is either 0 or 1 based on the comparison result. Since y is equal to z, value of the expression y == z becomes 1 and the value is assigned to x via the assignment operator.

Hence, the correct option is (B).

11. Comma acts as a separator here. The compiler creates an integer variable and initializes it with 1. The compiler fails to create integer variable 2 because 2 is not a valid identifier.

Hence, the correct option is (D).

12. The bracket operator has higher precedence than assignment operator. The expression within bracket operator is evaluated from left to right but it is always the result of the last expression which gets assigned.

Hence, the correct option is (B).

13. In the C programming language, the assignment operator (=) has higher precedence than the comma (,). In the given program, a comma act as a separator. The compiler creates an integer variable 'i' and initializes it with '1'. But, it fails to create integer variable '2' as '2' is not a valid identifier.

Hence, the correct option is (D).

14. Static functions can be called without any object. So the call "Test::getX()" is fine. Since x is initialized as 0, the first call to getX() returns 0. Note the statement x++ in constructor. When an array of 5 objects is created, the constructor is called 5 times. So x is incremented to 5 before the next call to getX().

Hence, the correct option is (C).

15. If a member variable is declared static, all objects of that class have access to a single instance of that variable. Static variables are sometimes called class variables, class fields, or class-wide fields because they don't belong to a specific object; they belong to the class. In the above code, static variable next_id is used to assign a unique id to all objects.

Hence, the correct option is (B).

16. The objects can be passed in three ways.

1. Pass by value
2. Pass by reference
3. Pass by address

Pass by value means you are making a copy in memory of the actual parameter's value that is passed in, a copy of the contents of the actual parameter.

Pass by reference of an argument in the calling function to the corresponding formal parameter of the called function. The called function can modify the value of the argument by using its reference passed in.

If you declare a formal parameter of a function as a pointer type, you are passing that parameter by its address. The pointer is copied, but not the data it points to. So, Pass By Address offers another method of allowing us to change the original argument of a function.

Hence, the correct option is (C).

17. When an object is passed by value, a new object is created implicitly. This new object uses the assignment of the implicit value, the same as that of the object being passed. Pass by value means you are making a copy in memory of the actual parameter's value that is passed in, a copy of the contents of the actual parameter. Use pass by value when when you are only "using" the parameter for some computation, not changing it for the client program.

Hence, the correct option is (A).

18. Pass by address uses the explicit address passing to the function whereas pass by reference implicitly passes the address of the object. When an object is passed by reference, its address is passed implicitly. This will make changes to the main function whenever any modification is done.

Hence, the correct option is (C).

19. If an object is passed by reference, the changes made in the function are reflected to the main object of caller function too. When an object is passed by reference, its address is passed implicitly. This will make changes to the main function whenever any modification is done. The objects can be passed by reference if required to use the same object. The values can be passed so that the main objective remains the same.

Hence, the correct option is (A).

20. Dynamic binding or runtime binding or late binding is that type of binding which happens at the execution time of the program or code. Function or method overriding is the perfect example of this type of binding. Virtual functions are used to achieve the concept of function overriding.

Hence, the correct option is (C).

21. The internet is a globally connected network system that uses TCP/IP to transmit data via various types of media. The internet is a network of global exchanges – including private, public, business, academic and government networks – connected by guided, wireless and fiber-optic technologies.

Hence, the correct option is (A).

22. A database is an organized collection of data, generally stored and accessed electronically from a computer system. Where databases are more complex they are often developed using formal design and modeling techniques

Hence, the correct option is (D).

23. A bus topology is a topology for a Local Area Network (LAN) in which all the nodes are connected to a single cable. The cable to which the nodes connect is called a "backbone". If the backbone is broken, the entire segment fails.

Hence, the correct option is (C).

24. Convergence occurs when all ports on bridges and switches have transitioned to either the forwarding or blocking states. No data is forwarded until convergence is complete. Before data can be forwarded again, all devices must be updated.

Hence, the correct option is (C).

25. WPA2 is a type of encryption used to secure the vast majority of Wi-Fi networks. A WPA2 network provides unique encryption keys for each wireless client that connects to it.

Hence, the correct option is (C).

26. DDL is short name of Data Definition Language, which deals with database schemas and descriptions, of how the data should reside in the database. Data Definition Language, used to perform all other essential tasks such as deleting relation and related schemas in defining the structure relation.

Hence, the correct option is (D).

27. DML provides the ability to query information from the database and insert tuples into, delete tuples from, and modify tuples in the database. A data manipulation language (DML) is a computer programming language used to store, retrieve, modify, and erase data from a database. DML stands for the Data Manipulation Language used to perform the required changes in the relation's values.

Hence, the correct option is (A).

28. The DBMS (or Database Management System) is a type of system software used for several operations such as creating tables/databases, storing data, managing databases. It also allows modifying the data stored in the database as well.

Hence, the correct option is (A).

29. A generalization is a bottom-up approach in which multiple lower-level entities are combined to form a single higher-level entity. Generalization is usually used to find common attributes among entities to form a generalized entity. As defined in the question the attributes of the Instructor Entity Set and the Secretary Entity Set.

Hence, the correct option is (C).

30. A functional dependency is a generalization of the notion of a key. It requires the value for a certain set of attributes to determine uniquely the value for another set of attributes.

Hence, the correct option is (A).

31. Join clause joins two tables by matching the common column.

Therefore, we can also use to the following code for join-

Select name, course_id from instructor natural join teaches;

Hence, the correct option is (B).

32. The Query given in option (D) does not contain the "from" clause, which specifies the relation from which the values have to be selected or fetched.

Hence, the correct option is (D).

33. In the above-given Query, the "%" (like) operator will be used, which is generally used while searching for a certain pattern in the strings. It represents the single and multiple characters. In this case, it used with "Where "louse to select the "dept_name" that contains the Computer Since as its ending string. To understand it more clearly, consider the following syntax:

Syntax

SELECT column1, column2, ...

FROM table_name

WHERE columnN LIKE pattern;

Hence, the correct option is (C).

34. External commands are required to perform various tasks in DOS. External commands are powerful. They help fix problems, improve performance, and perform other actions as well. External commands usually have higher resource requirements than internal commands. Keeping them in separate files, separated from internal commands, helps to reduce the load on Windows. They can also be added to Windows whenever needed by copying the external command's file to the computer.

Hence, the correct option is (B).

35. If you want to execute more than one program at a time, the systems software you are using must be capable of multitasking. Multitasking, in an operating system, is allowing a user to perform more than one computer task (such as the operation of an application program) at a time.

Hence, the correct option is (D).

36. The HTML DTD begins with a series of parameter entity definitions. A parameter entity definition defines a kind of macro that may be referenced and expanded elsewhere in the DTD. These macros may not appear in HTML documents, only in the DTD. Other types of macros, called character references, may be used in the text of an HTML document or within attribute values.

Hence, the correct option is (A).

37. The <br> tag in the HTML document is used to create a line break in a text. If we place the <br> tag in HTML code, then it works the same as pressing the enter key in a word processor.

Hence, the correct option is (A).

38. The <ul> tag in HTML is used to define the unordered list item in an HTML document. It contains the list items <li> element. The <ul> tag requires opening and closing tag. By using CSS style you can easily design unordered list.

Syntax:

<ul> list of items </ul>

Unordered list has 3 types of bulleted list:

- disc
- circle
- square

Hence, the correct option is (A).

39. RAD stands for Rapid Application Development. Rapid application development is an agile software development approach that focuses more on ongoing software projects and user feedback and less on following a strict plan. As such, it emphasizes rapid prototyping over costly planning.

Hence, the correct option is (A).

40. All of the above are valid step in SDLC framework. There are total 7 steps in SDLC framework:

1. Step 1: Project Planning: The first stage of SDLC is all about "What do we want?" Project planning is a vital role in the software delivery lifecycle since this is the part where the team estimates the cost and defines the requirements of the new software.
2. Step 2: Gathering Requirements & Analysis: The second step of SDLC is gathering maximum information from the client requirements for the product. Discuss each detail and specification of the product with the customer.
3. Step 3: Design: In the design phase (3rd step of SDLC), the program developer scrutinizes whether the prepared software suffices all the requirements of the end-user.
4. Step 4: Coding or Implementation: Time to code! It means translating the design to a computer-legible language. In this fourth stage of SDLC, the tasks are divided into modules or units and assigned to various developers. The developers will then start building the entire system by writing code using the programming languages they chose.
5. Step 5: Testing: Once the developers build the software, then it is deployed in the testing environment. Then the testing team tests the functionality of the entire system. In this fifth phase of SDLC, the testing is done to ensure that the entire application works according to the customer requirements.
6. Step 6: Deployment: The sixth phase of SDLC: Once the testing is done, and the product is ready for deployment, it is released for customers to use. The

size of the project determines the complexity of the deployment.

7. Step 7: Maintenance: The actual problem starts when the customer actually starts using the developed system and those needs to be solved from time to time. Maintenance is the seventh phase of SDLC where the developed product is taken care of. According to the changing user end environment or technology, the software is updated timely.

Hence, the correct option is (D).

Mock Test 02

Q.1 What will be the output of the following pseudo code for arr[]= 1,2,3,4,5

```
initialize i,n
intialize and array of size n
accept the values for the array
for o to n
arr[i] = arr[i]+arr[i+1]
end for
print the array elements
```

A. 3 5 7 6 5 **B.** 3 5 7 9 1 1
C. 3 5 9 1 5 2 0 **D.** error

Q.2 What will be the output of the following pseudo-code?

```
#include<stdio.h>
int fun(int x, int y);
int main()
{
int i,n;
i=5;
n=7;
int f = fun(5,7);
printf("%d", f);
}
int fun(int x, int y)
{
if(x<=0)
return y;
else
return(fun(x-1,y-1));
}
```

A. 0(zero) **B.** 1 **C.** 2 **D.** 3

Q.3 What will be the output of the following code:

```
#include <stdio.h>
#include <stdlib.h>
#define LIMIT 10 /*size of integers array*/
int main () {
  unsigned long long int i,j;
  int * primes;
  int z = 1;
  primes = malloc(sizeof(int)*LIMIT);
  for (i=2;i<LIMIT;i++)
    primes [i] = 1;
  for (i=2;i<LIMIT;i++)
    if (primes[i])
      for (j=i;i*j<LIMIT;j++)
        primes[i*j]=0;
  for (i=2;i<LIMIT;i++)
    if (primes[i])
      printf("%dth prime = %dn\n",z++,i);
  return 0;
}
```

A. None of the below

B.
1th prime - 2 n
2th prime - 3 n
3th prime - 5 n

C.
1th prime - 2 n
2th prime - 3 n
3th prime - 5 n
4th prime -7 n
5th prime -9 n
6th prime -11 n

D.
1th prime - 2 n
2th prime - 3 n
3th prime - 5 n
4th prime -7 n

Q.4 What will be the output of the following code snippet if the value of LIMIT = 10

```
#include <stdio.h>
#include <stdlib.h>
int main()
{
int m = 2, c=1;
int n,a,b, limit=10;
while(c< limit)
{
for (int n = 1; n< m; ++n)
{
a = m * m - n * n;
b = 2 * m * n;
c = m * m + n * n;
if (c >limit)
break;
printf("%d %d %d\n", a, b, c);
}
m++;
}
}
```

A. 157

B.
2 5 7
7 9 10

C.
1 2 3
4 5 6
7 8 9

D.
3 4 5
8 6 10

Q.5 What will be the output of the following code?

```
#include<stdio.h>
int main ()
{
 int n=5, k, f1, f2, f;
 if ( n < 2 )
  return n;
 else
 {
  f1 = f2 = 1;
  for(k=2;k<n;k++)
   {
    f = f1 + f2;
    f2 = f1;
    f1 = f;
```

```
    }
    printf("%d",f) ;
  }
}
```

A. 8 **B.** 5 **C.** 13 **D.** 7

Q.6 What is the 16-bit compiler allowable range for integer constants?

A. -3.4e38 to 3.4e38 **B.** -32767 to 32768
C. -32668 to 32667 **D.** -32768 to 32767

Q.7 What is required in each C program?

A. The program must have at least one function.
B. The program does not require any function.
C. Input data
D. Output data

Q.8 What will this program print?

```
main()
{
int i = 2;
{
int i = 4, j = 5;
printf("%d %d", i, j);
}
printf("%d %d", i, j);
}
```

A. 4 52 5 **B.** 2 52 5
C. 4 54 5 **D.** None of the these

Q.9 #include<userdefined.h>
Which of the following is the correct syntax to add the header file in the C++ program?

A. #include<userdefined>
B. #include "userdefined.h"
C. <include> "userdefined.h"
D. Both A and B

Q.10 Which of the following is the correct syntax to print the message in C++ language?

A. cout <<"Hello world!";
B. Cout << Hello world! ;
C. Out <<"Hello world!;
D. None of the above

Q.11 Which of the following is the correct identifier?

A. $var_name **B.** VAR_123
C. varname@ **D.** None of the above

Q.12 Study the following program:
print(print(print("Example")))
What will be the output of this program?

A. Example None None
B. None None Example
C. None Example None
D. Example

Q.13 Study the following program:
print(True ** False / True)
What will be the output of this program?

A. True ** False / True **B.** 1
C. 1 ** 0 / 1 **D.** None of the these

Q.14 Which of the following option leads to the portability and security of Java?

A. Bytecode is executed by JVM
B. The applet makes the Java code secure and portable
C. Use of exception handling
D. Dynamic binding between objects

Q.15 Which of the following is not a Java features?

A. Dynamic
B. Architecture Neutral
C. Use of pointers
D. Object-oriented

Q.16 When an object is returned by a function, a ___________ is automatically created to hold the return value.

A. Temporary object **B.** Virtual object
C. New object **D.** Data member

Q.17 Which among the following is not a member of the class?

A. Virtual function **B.** Const function
C. Static function **D.** Friend function

Q.18 How to overcome the problem arising due to the destruction of the temporary objects?

A. Overloading insertion operator
B. Overriding functions can be used
C. Overloading parenthesis or returning object
D. Overloading assignment operator and defining copy constructor

Q.19 How many objects can be returned at once?

A. Only 1 **B.** Only 2 **C.** Only 3 **D.** Only 4

Q.20 Which of the following language was developed as the first purely object programming language?

A. SmallTalk **B.** C++
C. Kotlin **D.** Java

Q.21 Complex networks today are made up of hundreds and sometimes thousands of _______.

A. Documents **B.** Components
C. Servers **D.** Entities

Q.22 The first Network is _________.

A. CNNET **B.** NSFNET
C. ASAPNET **D.** ARPANET

Q.23 A USB communication device that supports data encryption for secure wireless communication for notebook users is called a _____.

A. USB wireless network adapter
B. Wireless switch
C. Wireless hub
D. Router

Q.24 If you want to disable STP on a port connected to a server, which command would you use?

A. Disable spanning-tree
B. Spanning-tree off
C. Spanning-tree security
D. Spanning-tree portfast

Q.25 When a router is connected to a Frame Relay WAN link using a serial DTE interface, how is the clock rate determined?

A. Supplied by the CSU/DSU
B. By the far end router
C. By the clock rate command
D. By the Physical layer bitstream timing

Q.26 Which one of the following refers to the "data about data"?

A. Directory
B. Sub Data
C. Warehouse
D. Meta Data

Q.27 Which of the following refers to the level of data abstraction that describes exactly how the data actually stored?

A. Conceptual Level
B. Physical Level
C. File Level
D. Logical Level

Q.28 Which one of the following refers to the copies of the same data (or information) occupying the memory space at multiple places.

A. Data Repository
B. Data Inconsistency
C. Data Mining
D. Data Redundancy

Q.29 In general, a file is basically a collection of all related_____.

A. Rows and Columns
B. Fields
C. Database
D. Records

Q.30 The term "Data" refers to:

A. The electronic representation of the information(or data)
B. Basic information
C. Row Facts and figures
D. Row information

Q.31 Which of the following is not a valid SQL type?

A. FLOAT
B. NUMERIC
C. DECIMAL
D. CHARACTER

Q.32 In the following Query, which of the following can be placed in the Query's blank portion to display the salary from highest to lowest amount, and sorting the employs name alphabetically?

SELECT *
FROM instructor
ORDER BY salary ____, name ___;

A. Ascending, Descending
B. Asc, Desc
C. Desc, Asc
D. Descending, Ascending

Q.33 The given Query can be replaced with __________.

SELECT name
FROM instructor1
WHERE salary <= 100000 AND salary >= 90000;

A. SELECT name
FROM instructor1
WHERE salary BETWEEN 100000 AND 90000

B. SELECT name
FROM instructor|
WHERE salary BETWEEN 90000 AND 100000;

C. SELECT name
FROM instructor1
WHERE salary BETWEEN 90000 AND 100000;

D. SELECT name
FROM instructor!
WHERE salary <= 90000 AND salary>=100000;

Q.34 What type of scheduling is round-robin scheduling?

A. Linear data scheduling
B. Non-linear data scheduling
C. Preemptive scheduling
D. Non-preemptive scheduling

Q.35 What is the work of Round-robin scheduling?

A. It allows interactive tasks quicker access to the processor.
B. It is quite complex to implement.
C. It gives each task the same chance at the processor.
D. It allows processor-bound tasks more time in the processor.

Q.36 With which element width attribute is not define?

A. <input>
B. <object>
C. <embed>
D. <textarea>

Q.37 Which of the following tag is used to make the underlined text?

A. <i>
B. <ul>
C. <u>
D. <pre>

Q.38 How to create a checkbox in HTML?

A. <input type = "checkbox">
B. <input type = "button">
C. <checkbox>
D. <input type = "check">

Q.39 A descriptive and diagrammatic representation of software life cycle is called:

A. Software descriptive model
B. Software life cycle model
C. Software phases
D. Software phases

Q.40 Which of the following is not correct model in Software Development Paradigm?

A. Waterfall Model
B. P model
C. Spiral Model
D. V model

// Smart Answer Sheet //

Correct Indicates percentage of students who answered questions correctly.

Skipped Indicates percentage of students who skipped questions.

Q.	Ans.	Correct	Skipped
1	A	63.34 %	1.73 %
2	C	51.94 %	1.36 %
3	D	30.78 %	3.43 %
4	D	53.46 %	1.91 %
5	B	46.62 %	1.55 %
6	D	56.13 %	1.03 %
7	A	82.74 %	0.0 %
8	A	58.51 %	1.31 %
9	D	84.59 %	0.0 %
10	A	84.58 %	0.0 %
11	B	81.29 %	0.0 %
12	A	80.57 %	0.0 %
13	B	88.14 %	0.0 %
14	A	65.49 %	1.65 %
15	C	47.38 %	1.83 %
16	A	62.64 %	1.35 %
17	D	62.02 %	1.14 %
18	D	51.98 %	1.38 %
19	A	78.26 %	0.0 %
20	A	57.81 %	1.78 %
21	B	77.34 %	0.0 %
22	D	83.95 %	0.0 %
23	A	52.17 %	1.07 %
24	D	48.79 %	1.85 %
25	A	58.64 %	1.83 %
26	D	85.52 %	0.0 %
27	B	69.82 %	1.02 %
28	D	66.44 %	1.58 %
29	D	85.03 %	0.0 %
30	C	76.42 %	0.0 %
31	C	67.03 %	1.72 %
32	C	30.71 %	4.85 %
33	C	17.69 %	4.71 %
34	C	48.16 %	1.3 %
35	C	45.36 %	1.16 %
36	D	52.7 %	1.12 %
37	C	87.73 %	0.0 %
38	A	87.82 %	0.0 %
39	B	58.57 %	1.33 %
40	B	45.12 %	1.88 %

Performance Analysis	
Avg. Score (%)	55.0%
Toppers Score (%)	75.0%
Your Score	

//Hints and Solutions//

1. The following pseudo-code will add the first element with the second, the second element with the third, the third element with the fourth and the fourth element with the fifth, the fifth element will remain as it is and So, the output will be 3 5 7 9 5.

Hence, the correct option is (A).

2. This is a recursive code the function fun(int x, int y) will keep on calling itself until the value of x becomes zero, and when the base condition executes it will print the value of y.

Since the value of x is 5 and it is getting decremented by 1 on every function call and the value of y is also getting decremented by 1 on every function call. On the execution of the base condition, the value of x will become 0(as it has been decremented by 1, 5 times) and the value of y will become 2(as it is also has been decremented by 1, 5 times) and hence the output will be 2.

Hence, the correct option is (C).

3. The following code calculated the Prime Number upto the given range using the concept of Sieve method,

The sieve of Eratosthenes is an ancient algorithm for finding all prime numbers up to any given limit. It does so by iteratively marking as composite the multiples of each prime, starting with the first prime number, 2.

So, the output is:

1th prime - 2 n

2th prime - 3 n

3th prime - 5 n

4th prime -7 n

Hence, the correct option is (D).

4. The following code snippet generated Pythagorean triplets upto the given LIMIT.

So. the output is:

3 4 5

8 6 10

Hence, the correct option is (D).

5. The following code is generating Fibonacci series and returning the nth term.

So, the output is 5.

Hence, the correct option is (B).

6. In a 16-bit C compiler, we have 2 bytes to store the value.

- The range for signed integers is -32768 to 32767.
- The range for unsigned integers is 0 to 65535.
- The range for unsigned character is 0 to 255.

Hence, the correct option is (D).

7. Any C program has at least one function, and even the most trivial programs can specify additional functions. A function is a piece of code. In other words, it works like a sub-program.

Hence, the correct option is (A).

8. In this program, it will first print the inner value of the function and then print the outer value of the function.

So, the output is 4 52 5.

Hence, the correct option is (A).

9. To include the herder files in the C++ program user can use any of the following given syntax.

#include <Filename.h>

Hence, the correct option is (D).

10. To print the message in the C++ language user can use the following syntax:

```
#include <iostream>

using namespace std;
int main() {
cout<< "Hello World!";
cout<< "I am learning C++";
return 0;
}
```

Hence, the correct option is (A).

11. There are some certain rules that must be followed by the users while writing the identifiers.

- It may contain uppercase/lowercase letters, digits, and underscore (_) only.
- It always starts only with non-digit characters.
- It should not contain any special characters like $, @etc.

Hence, the correct option is (B).

12. In this program, the inner print function will run first as compared to the outer print function. Therefore, the correct output of this program is "Example None None".

Hence, the correct option is (A).

13. Binary values

True = 1

False = 0

(1 ** 0 / 1) = (10/ 1) = 1

Therefore, 1 is the correct output of the given program.

Hence, the correct option is (B).

14. The output of the Java compiler is bytecode, which leads to the security and portability of the Java code. It is a highly developed set of instructions that are designed to be executed by the Java runtime system known as Java Virtual Machine (JVM). The Java programs executed by the JVM that makes the code portable and secure. Because JVM prevents the code from generating its side effects. The Java code is portable, as the same byte code can run on any platform.

Hence, the correct option is (A).

15. The Java language does not support pointers; some of the major reasons are listed below:

- One of the major factors of not using pointers in Java is security concerns. Due to pointers, most of the users consider C-language very confusing and complex. This is the reason why Green Team (Java Team members) has not introduced pointers in Java.
- Java provides an effective layer of abstraction to the developers by not using pointers in Java.

Java is dynamic, architecture-neutral, and object-oriented programming language.

Hence, the correct option is (C).

16. When an object is returned by a function, a temporary object is automatically created to hold the return value. The values get assigned as required, and the temporary object gets destroyed. The temporary object is used to copy the values to another object or to be used in some way. The object holds all the values of the data members of the object.

Hence, the correct option is (A).

17. The public member functions of a class can easily access the private data members of the same class. This is achieved by the "friend", which is a non-member function to the class. Its private data can be accessed. That's why the friend function is not a member of the class.

Hence, the correct option is (D).

18. The problem arising due to the destruction of the temporary objects can be solved by overloading the assignment operator to get the values that might be getting returned while the destructor free the dynamic memory. Defining copy constructors can help us to do this in an even simpler way.

Hence, the correct option is (D).

19. Like any other value, only one object can be returned at ones. The only possible way to return more than one object is to return the address of an object array. But that again comes under returning object pointer.

Hence, the correct option is (A).

20. SmallTalk the language was developed as the first purely object programming language. This programming language was invented as the first pure OOPS (object-oriented) language. This language was designed by Alan Kay in the early 1970s.

Hence, the correct option is (A).

21. Complex networks today are made up of hundreds and sometimes thousands of components. For the effective functioning of these thousands of components, good network management is essential.

Hence, the correct option is (B).

22. The first network component, ARPANET, became operational in October 1969. The Advanced Research Projects Agency Network (ARPANET) was an early packet-switching network and the first network to implement the protocol suite TCP/IP. Both technologies became the technical foundation of the Internet.

Hence, the correct option is (D).

23. USB wireless network adapter is a communication device that plugs into a USB port and usually provides an intuitive graphical user interface (GUI) for easy configuration. It supports data encryption for secure wireless communication and is perfect for the traveler and notebook user.

Hence, the correct option is (A).

24. If you have a server or other devices connected into your switch that you're totally sure won't create a switching loop if STP is disabled, you can use something called **portfast** on these ports. Using it means the port won't spend the usual 50 seconds to come up while STP is converging.

Hence, the correct option is (D).

25. Clocking on a serial interface is always provided by the CSU/DSU (DCE device). However, if you do not have a CSU/DSU in your nonproduction test environment, then you need to supply clocking with the clock rate command on the serial interface of the router with the DCE cable attached.

Hence, the correct option is (A).

26. The Mata Data refers to the type of data that describes the other data or information. Simply defined, metadata is the summary and the description about your data that is used to classify, organize, label and understand data, making sorting and searching for data much easier.

Hence, the correct option is (D).

27. Data abstraction means displaying or sharing only the data that is needed and hiding from all other data until it is necessary to share it. However, the data abstraction level that describes how the data was actually stored in the user's machine (or system) is known as the Physical level.

Hence, the correct option is (B).

28. Data redundancy generally occurs whenever more than one copy of the exact same data exists in several different places. Sometimes it may cause data inconsistency, which can result in an unreliable source of data or information that is not good for anyone.

Hence, the correct option is (D).

29. Whenever we have some related data, information or records, we collect all those related data (or records), put them together, store them in one place, and give that collection a name that is known as a file.

Hence, the correct option is (D).

30. In general, the term "data" refers to the row facts and figures, whereas the information referred to as the data, which is really important for someone or a particular person.

Hence, the correct option is (C).

31. DECIMAL is not a valid SQL type because it is nothing but numeric only in SQL.

NUMERIC has fixed precision, and scale numbers range from -10^38+1 to 10^38-1.

FLOAT has floating precision number ranges from -1.79E + 308 to 1.79E + 308.

CHARACTER is a fixed-width character string data type that can be up to 8000 characters.

Hence, the correct option is (C).

32. To sort the salary from highest to lowest amount and display the employee's name alphabetically, one can use the "Desc and Asc" in the above-given Query.

Hence, the correct option is (C).

33. The "SQL" contains a comparison known as the "BETWEEN," which is also used in one of the given queries, as you can see. The "BETWEEN" operator is generally used to simplify the "WHERE" clause that is used to specify that the value is greater than one value or greater than some values, less than one or more values.

Hence, the correct option is (C).

34. Round-robin scheduling is a preemptive scheduling algorithm in which a specific time is provided to execute each process. This specific time is called time-slice.

Round Robin is a CPU scheduling algorithm where each process is assigned a fixed time slot in a cyclic way.

- It is simple, easy to implement, and starvation-free as all processes get lair share of CPU.
- One of the most commonly used technique in CPU scheduling as a core.
- It is preemptive as processes are assigned CPU only for a fixed slice of time at most.
- The disadvantage of it is more overhead of context switching.

Hence, the correct option is (C).

35. Round-robin scheduling gives each task the same chance at the processor. Round Robin is a CPU scheduling algorithm where each process is assigned a fixed time slot in a cyclic way. It is simple, easy to implement, and starvation-free as all processes get a fair share of CPU. One of the most commonly used techniques in CPU scheduling is a core.

Hence, the correct option is (C).

36. width attribute is defined with <object>, <iframe>, <img>, <video>, <canvas>, <embed>, <input>. <textarea> is used commonly with autofocus, cols, dirname, disabled, form, maxlength, minlength, name, placeholder, readonly, rows and many other attributes.

Hence, the correct option is (D).

37. The <u> (underline tag) tag in HTML is used to display the underlined text. It rendered as a solid underlined text, but it can be changed using CSS properties.

Hence, the correct option is (C).

38. To create a checkbox in HTML, we have to use the <input> tag and give the value checkbox to its type attribute. The <input type="checkbox"> defines a checkbox. The checkbox is shown as a square box that is ticked (checked) when activated. Checkboxes are used to let a user select one or more options of a limited number of choices.

Hence, the correct option is (A).

39. Software life cycle model is a descriptive and diagrammatic representation of software life cycle. A software development life cycle (SDLC) model is a conceptual framework describing all activities in a software development project from planning to maintenance. This process is associated with several models, each including a variety of tasks and activities.

Hence, the correct option is (B).

40. P-Modeling Framework is a package of guidelines, methods, tools and templates for the development process improvement. P-Modeling framework can be integrated into any other SDLC in use, e.g., MSF Agile, MSF CMMI, RUP, etc. Rest all are model in Software Development Paradigm.

Hence, the correct option is (B).

Mock Test 03

Q.1 What purporse does the following code serves?

```
int main()
{
int array[] = {5, 3, 1, 9, 8, 2, 4, 7};
int size = sizeof(array)/sizeof(array[0]);
int i, j, min_idx,temp;
for (i = 0; i< size-1; i++)
{
min_idx = i;
for (j = i+1; j< size; j++)
{
if (array[j]< array[min_idx])
min_idx = j;
}
temp = array[min_idx];
array[min_idx] = array[i];
array[i] = temp;}
```

A. Finds some specific element in the array
B. Sort the elements of array
C. Find the smallest element in the array
D. None of the above

Q.2 What operation does the following pseudo code performs?

```
Declare an array of string type variable called word
Declare a loopcounter
Store a string in the array word
for loopcounter = (length of the word) – 1 to 0
loopcounter = loopcounter – 1
print arrayword[loopcounter]
endfor
Algorithm end
```

A. It accepts a string.
B. It reverses the string.
C. It prints the string in the same order.
D. None of the above

Q.3 What will be the value of s if n=127?

```
Read n
i=0
s=0
n = 127
Function Sample(int n)
while(n >0):
r = n % 10
p = 8 ^ i
s = s + p * r
i += 1
n = n / 10
return s:
End Function
s=Sample(n)
```

A. 27 **B.** 187 **C.** 87 **D.** 120

Q.4 What will be the value of s if N=20?

```
Read N
Function sample(N)
s = 0
f = 1
i = 1
while i<= N:
f = f * i
s = s +(i / f)
i+=1
End while
return(s);
End Function
```

A. 3.789456
B. 2.7182818284590455
C. 80.35741
D. 2.7182817184590455

Q.5 What would be the output of the following pseudocode?

```
Integer a, b, c
Set a = 8, b = 51, c = 2
c = (a ^ c)^ (a)
b = b mod 4
Print a + b + c
```

A. 13 **B.** 17 **C.** 26 **D.** 16

Q.6 What is a lint?

A. C compiler
B. Interactive debugger
C. Analyzing tool
D. C interpreter

Q.7 Study the following program:

```
main()
{
int a = 1, b = 2, c = 3;
printf("%d", a + = (a + = 3, 5, a));
}
```

What will be the output of this program?

A. 6 **B.** 9 **C.** 12 **D.** 8

Q.8 Which one of the following is a loop construct that will always be executed once?

A. For **B.** While
C. Switch **D.** Do while

Q.9 Directives are translated by the-

A. Pre-processor **B.** Compiler
C. Linker **D.** Editor

Q.10 The C++ language is _____ object-oriented language.

A. Pure Object oriented
B. Not Object oriented
C. Semi Object-oriented or Partial Object-oriented
D. None of the above

Q.11 Study the following function:

```
all([2,4,0,6])
```

What will be the output of this function?

A. False **B.** True
C. 0 **D.** Invalid code

Q.12 Which of the following comment syntax is correct to create a single-line comment in the C++ program?

A. //Comment **B.** /Comment/
C. Comment// **D.** None of the above

Q.13 What should be the execution order, if a class has a method, static block, instance block, and constructor, as shown below?

```
public class First_C {
public void myMethod()
{
System.out.println("Method");
}
{
System.out.println(" Instance Block");
}
public void First_C()
{
System.out.println("Constructor ");
}
static {
System.out.println("static block");
}
public static void main(String[] args) {
First_C c = new First_C();
c.First_C();
c.myMethod();
}
}
```

A. Instance block, method, static block, and constructor
B. Method, constructor, instance block, and static block
C. Static block, method, instance block, and constructor
D. Static block, instance block, constructor, and method

Q.14 What will be the output of the following program?

```
public class MyFirst {
public static void main(String[] args) {
MyFirst obj = new MyFirst(n);
}
static int a = 10;
static int n;
int b = 5;
int c;
public MyFirst(int m) {
System.out.println(a + ", " + b + ", " + c + ", " + n + ", " + m);
}
// Instance Block
{
b = 30;
n = 20;
}
// Static Block
static
{
a = 60;
}
}
```

A. 10, 5, 0, 20, 0 **B.** 10, 30, 20
C. 60, 5, 0, 20 **D.** 60, 30, 0, 20, 0

Q.15 The \u0021 article referred to as a-

A. Unicode escape sequence
B. Octal escape
C. Hexadecimal
D. Line feed

Q.16 Which of the following class is known as the generic class?

A. Final class **B.** Template class
C. Abstract class **D.** Efficient code

Q.17 Define the programming language, which does not support all types of inheritance?

A. Smalltalk **B.** Kotlin
C. Java **D.** C++

Q.18 If there is an abstract method in a class then, ______________.

A. Class must be abstract class
B. Class may or may not be abstract class
C. Class is generic
D. Class must be public

Q.19 Which two features of object-oriented programming are the same?

A. Abstraction and Polymorphism features are the same.
B. Inheritance and Encapsulation features are the same.
C. Encapsulation and Polymorphism features are the same.
D. Encapsulation and Abstraction.

Q.20 Who developed object-oriented programming?

A. Adele Goldberg **B.** Dennis Ritchie
C. Alan Kay **D.** Andrea Ferro

Q.21 Which NetWare protocol works on layer 3 - network layer - of the OSI model?

A. IPX **B.** NCP
C. SPX **D.** NetBIOS

Q.22 Which of the following is true regarding VTP?

A. All switches are VTP servers by default.
B. All switches are VTP transparent by default.
C. VTP is on by default with a domain name of Cisco on all Cisco switches.
D. All switches are VTP clients by default.

Q.23 In which method we can connect to internet?

A. Dial-up **B.** SLIP
C. PPP **D.** All of these

Q.24 The three types of IP addresses are:

A. Network Address, Host Address, Local Address
B. Network Address, Host Address, Broad Cast Address
C. Network Address, Host Address, Packet Address
D. Network Address, Host Address, Frame Address

Q.25 A network that needs human beings to manually route signals is called:

A. Fiber Optic Network
B. Bus Network
C. T-switched network
D. Ring network

Q.26 Rows of a relation are known as the ______.

A. Degree **B.** Tuples
C. Entity **D.** All of the above

Q.27 Which of the following refers to the number of tuples in a relation?

A. Entity **B.** Column
C. Cardinality **D.** Aggregation

Q.28 The term "DFD" stands for?

A. Data file diagram **B.** Data flow document
C. Data flow diagram **D.** None of the above

Q.29 Which of the following is a top-down approach in which the entity's higher level can be divided into two lower sub-entities?

A. Aggregation **B.** Generalization
C. Specialization **D.** Relation

Q.30 In which one of the following, the multiple lower entities are grouped (or combined) together to form a single higher-level entity?

A. Specialization **B.** Generalization
C. Aggregation **D.** Transaction

Q.31 Which of the following is not a DDL command?

A. TRUNCATE **B.** ALTER
C. CREATE **D.** UPDATE

Q.32 Which of the following are TCL commands?

A. COMMIT and ROLLBACK
B. UPDATE and TRUNCATE
C. SELECT and INSERT
D. GRANT and REVOKE

Q.33 Which statement is used to delete all rows in a table without having the action logged?

A. DELETE **B.** REMOVE
C. DROP **D.** TRUNCATE

Q.34 What is the name of the system which deals with the running of the actual computer and not with the programming problems?

A. Operating system **B.** Systems program
C. Object program **D.** Source program

Q.35 What is the initial value of the semaphore to allow only one of the many processes to enter their critical section?

A. 8 **B.** 1 **C.** 16 **D.** 0

Q.36 Which of the following tag is used to add rows in the table?

A. <td> and </td> **B.** <th> and </th>
C. <tr> and </tr> **D.** None of the above

Q.37 The <hr> tag in HTML is used for-

A. New line **B.** Vertical ruler
C. New paragraph **D.** Horizontal ruler

Q.38 Which of the following attribute is used to provide a unique name to an element?

A. Class **B.** Id
C. Type **D.** None of the above

Q.39 Build & Fix Model is suitable for programming exercises of _________ LOC (Line of Code).

A. 100-200 **B.** 300-400
C. 600-700 **D.** Above 800+

Q.40 Match the following-

1	Waterfall model	a)	Specifications can be developed incrementally
2	Evolutionary model	b)	Requirements compromises are inevitable
3	Component-based software engineering	c)	Explicit recognition of risk
4	Spiral development	d)	Inflexible partitioning of the project into stages

A. 1 – a, 2 – b, 3 – c, 4 - d
B. 1 – d, 2 – a, 3 – b, 4 - c
C. 1 – d, 2 – d, 3 – a, 4 - c
D. 1 – c, 2 – a, 3 – b, 4 - d

// Smart Answer Sheet //

Correct — Indicates percentage of students who answered questions correctly.

Skipped — Indicates percentage of students who skipped questions.

Q.	Ans.	Correct	Skipped
1	B	46.07 %	1.88 %
2	B	47.12 %	1.82 %
3	C	55.7 %	1.51 %
4	B	54.04 %	1.68 %
5	A	70.0 %	1.16 %
6	C	54.49 %	1.11 %
7	D	44.06 %	1.5 %
8	D	55.16 %	1.3 %
9	A	53.74 %	1.48 %
10	C	66.07 %	1.91 %
11	A	83.89 %	0.0 %
12	A	69.44 %	1.68 %
13	D	54.64 %	1.74 %
14	D	49.24 %	1.68 %
15	A	40.48 %	1.86 %
16	B	76.36 %	0.0 %
17	C	84.99 %	0.0 %
18	A	67.15 %	1.44 %
19	D	60.1 %	1.23 %
20	C	85.27 %	0.0 %
21	A	69.89 %	1.79 %
22	A	50.31 %	1.23 %
23	D	57.86 %	1.74 %
24	B	62.84 %	1.2 %
25	C	63.92 %	1.55 %
26	B	80.93 %	0.0 %
27	C	42.09 %	1.81 %
28	C	69.74 %	1.64 %
29	C	65.71 %	1.19 %
30	B	53.51 %	1.64 %
31	D	84.65 %	0.0 %
32	A	64.11 %	1.28 %
33	D	42.07 %	1.79 %
34	B	42.79 %	1.03 %
35	B	44.45 %	1.59 %
36	C	85.01 %	0.0 %
37	D	84.52 %	0.0 %
38	B	58.55 %	1.94 %
39	A	50.62 %	1.61 %
40	B	14.02 %	4.47 %

Performance Analysis	
Avg. Score (%)	62.5%
Toppers Score (%)	72.5%
Your Score	

//Hints and Solutions//

1. Following code snippet is the code of selection sort, which compares each element of the array with all the other elements and arrange them in a specific order. instead of starting at index 1 you would start at index 0. The code doesn't have to check the value of the minValue (array[temp] in the code) vs the value at the index, instead you just always swap the minValue and the value at the index (this will be safe if the range of values you previously checked for your minValue includes the value at the index).

Hence, the correct option is (B).

2. The following pseudo code prints the entered string in the reverse order. We have used a reverse for loop, for reverse printing the string.

In the above code, length of the word is declare as a string.

The above code is define as (length of the word) – 1 to 0, that is in reversible order.

For example:

length of the word=10

Then, the output is {9, 8, 7, 6, 5, 4, 3, 2, 1, 0}.

Hence, the correct option is (B).

3. The following code is converting an octal number into its decimal representation. Here we are treating 127 as an octal input and converting it into its decimal representation that is 87.

Hence, the correct option is (C).

4. Loop will end up giving output as 2.7182818284590455 as value of f is initialized to 1 and then following BODMAS rule the next step "s = s +(i / f)" will be followed and i is incremented.

Hence, the correct option is (B).

5. There are three variables a, b and c declared. Value initialized for a is 8, b is 51 and c is 2.

When we do a bitwise exclusive OR of (8^2), the answer is 10. Again 10 bitwise exclusive OR of a i.e (10 ^ 8) is 2, which will be stored in variable c.

Then taking modulo operation for b by 4 (b%4) the answer is 3.

Finally adding all the updated values of a,b, and c (8+2+3) and the output of Pseudocode is 13.

E.g. code to explain this:

```
int main()
{
int a=8,b=51,c=2;
c = (a ^ c)^ (a); =>(8^2) ^(8) =>10 ^ 8 =>2
b = b % 4; =>3
cout<8+2+3 =>13
}
```

Hence, the correct option is (A).

6. Lint is an analyzing tool that analyzes the source code by suspicious constructions, stylistic errors, bugs, and flag programming errors. Lint is a compiler-like tool in which it parses the source files of C programming. It checks the syntactic accuracy of these files.

Hence, the correct option is (C).

7. It is an effect of the comma operator.
a + = (a + = 3, 5, a)
It first evaluates to "a + = 3" i.e. a = a + 3 then evaluate 5 and then evaluate "a".
Therefore, we will get the output is 4.
Then,
a + = 4
It gives 8 as the output.

Hence, the correct option is (D).

8. The body of a loop is often executed at least once during the do-while loop. Once the body is performed, the condition is tested. If the condition is valid, it will execute the body of a loop; otherwise, control is transferred out of the loop.

Hence, the correct option is (D).

9. In C language, the pre-processor is a macro processor that is dynamically used by the C programmer to modify the program before it is properly compiled (Before construction, pro-processor directives are implemented).

Hence, the correct option is (A).

10. The common thing about the Pure Object-oriented language it provides three basic features like Inheritance, Encapsulation, and Polymorphism. Each programming language that supports these entire three features is known as the Pure-Object oriented language. Whereas if a programming language support all these three features but not support completely are known as the Partial-Object oriented languages or the Semi Object-oriented languages.

The main reasons why the C++ programming language is Known as Semi-Object oriented language are as follows:

1. Availability of the Friend function-

A friend class is allowed to access private and protected members of another class, within which it is declared a friend. It may be very useful for some time, but still, it violates the rule of the Object-Oriented features.

2. Concept of the Global variable-

As we all know that we can declare a global variable in C++ language that can be easily accessible from anywhere within the program. So again, C++ does not provide complete privacy because no one is restricted to access and manipulate that data/information. Hence it offers partial Encapsulation, unlike Java Language, in which a user only allows to declare a variable within the class and can provide access specifier to it.

3. The main function is Out-side the class-

C++ is an object-oriented language, but still, object-oriented is not fundamentally related (or implicit) to the language. So a user can easily write a valid, well-defined C++ code even without using any object once.

Hence, the correct option is (C).

11. If any element is zero, it returns a false value, and if all elements are non-zero, it returns a true value. Therefore, the output of this "all([2,4,0,6])" function will be false.

Hence, the correct option is (D).

12. To create a single line comment (or one-line comment) in C++ program one can use the "// write comment" syntax. We can understand it more easily with the help of following given Program

Example

```
#include <stdio.h>

int main(void)
{
// This is a single line comment
// Welcome user comment
printf("Welcome to Javatpoint");
return 0;
}
```

Hence, the correct option is (A).

13. The order of execution is:

1. The static block will execute whenever the class is loaded by JVM.
2. Instance block will execute whenever an object is created, and they are invoked before the constructors. For example, if there are two objects, the instance block will execute two times for each object.
3. The constructor will execute after the instance block, and it also execute every time the object is created.
4. A method is always executed at the end.

Hence, the correct option is (D).

14. In the above code, there are two values of variable a, i.e., 10 and 60. Similarly, there are two values of variable b, i.e., 5 and 30. But in the output, the values of a and b are 60 and 30, respectively. It is because of the execution order of the program.

The execution order of the program is that the static block executes first, then instance block, and then constructor. Hence, the JVM will consider the value of a and b as 60 and 30 concerning the execution order. The value of a = 10 and b = 5 are of no use. And the value of variables c and m is 0 as we have not assigned any value to them.

Hence, the correct option is (D).

15. In Java, Unicode characters can be used in string literals, comments, and commands, and are expressed by Unicode Escape Sequences. A Unicode escape sequence is made up of the following articles:

- A backslash '\' (ASCII character 92)
- A 'u' (ASCII 117)
- One or more additional 'u' characters that are optional.
- A four hexadecimal digits (a character from 0 - 9 or a-f or A-F)

Hence, the correct option is (A).

16. Template classes are those classes which can be used for any value of data type. So, these are known as a generic class. Template classes help in making the genetic classes and generate the objects of classes based on the parameters. This type of class also saves system memory.

Hence, the correct option is (B).

17. Java is a programming language that disapproves of the concept of 'multiple inheritance'. So, it does not support with all types of inheritance. But, we can implement 'multiple inheritance' in Java language using the interface concept.

Hence, the correct option is (C).

18. It is a rule that if a class have even one abstract method, it must be an abstract class. If this rule was not made, the abstract methods would have got skipped to get defined in some places which are undesirable with the idea of abstract class.

Hence, the correct option is (A).

19. Encapsulation and Abstraction are the same OOPS concepts. Encapsulation hides the features of the object and binds all the properties inside a single class. And abstraction is a feature that shows the required data to the user.

Hence, the correct option is (D).

20. In the year 1970, Alan Kay gave Object-Oriented programming. He coined the concept of OOPS at a grad school in the year 1966 or 1967. Alan kay, Adele Goldberg, Dan Ingalls and others developed the first Smalltalk programming language, which follows the OOPS concept.

Hence, the correct option is (C).

21. IPX (Internetwork Packet Exchange) is the NetWare network layer 3 protocol used for transferring information on LANs that use Novell's NetWare. IPX is a networking protocol that conducts the activities and affairs of the end-to-end process of timely, managed and secured data. Originally used by the Novell NetWare operating system and it was later adopted by Windows.

Hence, the correct option is (A).

22. All Cisco switches are VTP servers by default. No other VTP information is configured on a Cisco switch by default. You must set the VTP domain name on all switches to be the same domain name or they will not share the VTP database.

Hence, the correct option is (A).

23. Dial-up Internet access is a form of Internet access that uses the facilities of the public switched telephone network to establish a connection to an Internet service provider by dialing a telephone number on a conventional telephone line.SLIP (Serial Line Internet Protocol) is the result of the integration of modem protocols prior to the suite of TCP/IP protocols. Point-to-Point

Protocol (PPP) is a data link layer communications protocol used to establish a direct connection between two nodes.

Hence, the correct option is (D).

24. Host address is the portion of the address used to identify hosts and network address is an identifier for a node or network interface of a telecommunications network. The broadcast address represents all devices of the network. If an IP packet is sent on a broadcast address, it is intended for all devices of that network.

Hence, the correct option is (B).

25. A network that needs human beings to manually route signals is called a T-switched network. A network switch is a computer networking device. T-switched networks route messages automatically among devices statement is False. A network switch (also called switching hub, bridging hub, officially MAC bridge) is a computer networking device that connects devices together on a computer network by using packet switching to receive, process, and forward data to the destination device.

Hence, the correct option is (C).

26. In relational data model, relations are saved in the format of Tables. This format stores the relation among entities. A table has rows and columns, where rows represents records and columns represent the attributes. A single row of a table, which contains a single record for that relation is called a tuple.

Hence, the correct option is (B).

27. Cardinality refers to the number of tuples of relation because cardinality represents the number of tuples in a relation.

To understand it in more detail, consider the following given example:

Suppose we have a relation (or table) that contains 30 tuples (or Rows) and four columns, so the cardinality of our relationship will be 30.

Hence, the correct option is (C).

28. The term "DFD" stands for the Data Flow Diagram. A data flow diagram shows the way information flows through a process or system. It includes data inputs and outputs, data stores, and the various sub-processes the data moves through. DFDs are built using standardized symbols and notation to describe various entities and their relationships.

Hence, the correct option is (C).

29. In specialization, the top-down approach is used, and it is apposite to the generalization.

In specialization, the higher-level entity can be divided into sub lower entities. It is generally used for identifying the subset of an entity set which share the distinguishing characteristics.

To understand it more clearly, consider the following example:

Suppose you have an entity, e.g., A vehicle. So through the specialization, you can be divided further into sub-entities like two-wheelers and four-wheelers.

Hence, the correct option is (C).

30. The bottom-up approach is used in the generalization. The several lower-level sub-entities are grouped together to make an individual higher-level entity. In short, we can say that it is totally the opposite of specialization.

To understand it more clearly, consider the following example:

Suppose you have several lower entities like bus, car, motorbike etc. So, in order to make a more generalize (or higher level) entity, you can combine them under a new higher-level entity such as a vehicle.

Hence, the correct option is (B).

31. UPDATE command is not a DDL command. An UPDATE command is used for managing the data stored in a database. It is an example of a DML command that also includes the INSERT and DELETE commands.

DDL commands are used to define the structure of the database, table, schemas, etc. It enables us to perform the operations like CREATE, DROP, ALTER, RENAME, and TRUNCATE schema objects.

Hence, the correct option is (D).

32. TCL stands for Transaction Control Commands used for managing the changes made by DML commands like INSERT, DELETE, and UPDATE. The TCL commands are automatically committed in the database; that's why we cannot use them directly while creating tables or dropping them.

Hence, the correct option is (A).

33. TRUNCATE statement removes all rows in a table without logging the individual row deletions. It uses fewer system and transaction log resources, which makes its execution fast. This statement is similar to the DELETE statement without the WHERE clause.

Hence, the correct option is (D).

34. Systems program deals with the running of the actual computer and not with the programming problems. A system program is a collection of instructions that performs a specific task when executed by a computer. System Programming can be defined as the act of building Systems Software using System Programming Languages. According to Computer Hierarchy, one which comes at last is Hardware. Then it is Operating System, System Programs, and finally Application Programs.

Hence, the correct option is (B).

35. The initial value of the semaphore to allow only one of the many processes to enter their critical section is 1 .

A semaphore is as an object with an integer value that we can manipulate with two routines. Because the initial value of the semaphore determines its behavior, before calling any other routine to interact with the semaphore. we declare a semaphore s and initialize it to the value of 1 .

A semaphore is a variable or abstract data type used to control access to a common resource by multiple processes in a concurrent system such as a multitasking operating system. A semaphore is simply a variable. This variable is used to solve critical section problems and to achieve process synchronization in the multiprocessing environment.

Hence, the correct option is (B).

36. The <tr> tag in HTML is used to define the rows in the table. It can consist one or more <th> head cells and <td> data cells to define a single row of HTML table.

Example:

```
<table>
  <tr>    <td></td>    <td></td>
  </tr>
<\table>
```

There are <tr>,</tr> is use for row in table. And <td>,</td> is used for column.

Hence, the correct option is (C).

37. The <hr> tag is used to specify a paragraph-level thematic break in HTML document. It is called a horizontal rule and draws a horizontal line. It is a self closing tag.

Example:

```
<html>
  <body>
    <p>This is a horizontal rule above this paragraph.</p>
    <hr>
  </body>
</html>
```

Hence, the correct option is (D).

38. The id attribute specifies a unique id/name for an HTML element. The value of the id attribute must be unique within the HTML document.

The id attribute is used to point to a specific style declaration in a style sheet. It is also used by JavaScript to access and manipulate the element with the specific id.

The syntax for id is: write a hash character (#), followed by an id name. Then, define the CSS properties within curly braces {}.

Example:

```
<html>
<head>
<style>
#myHeader {
  background-color: lightblue;
  color: black;
  padding: 40px;
  text-align: center;
}
</style>
</head>
<body>
<h1 id="myHeader">My Header</h1>
</body>
</html>
```

Hence, the correct option is (B).

39. Build & Fix Model is suitable for small projects & programming exercises of 100 or 200 lines. In the build and fix model (also referred to as an ad hoc model), the software is developed without any specification or design. An initial product is built, which is then repeatedly modified until it (software) satisfies the user. That is, the software is developed and delivered to the user.

Hence, the correct option is (A).

40. The correct match is 1 – d, 2 – a, 3 – b, 4 - c.

Waterfall Model: Moving forward compulsorily, it is impossible to go back to previous project phase in waterfall model. Hence, this method is inflexible.

Evolutionary: The model keeps changing with time and according to requirements. Hence, it is incremental in nature.

Component based: This model relies on reuse-based approach to defining, implementing and composing loosely coupled independent components into systems.

Spiral: This model is the most advanced. It includes four phases - Planning, Risk Analysis, Engineering and Evaluation.

Hence, the correct option is (B).

Mock Test 04

Q.1 Consider the following piece of code. What will be the space required for this code?

```
int sum (int A[], int n)
{
int sum = 0, i;
for (i = 0; i< n; i++)
sum = sum + A[i];
return sum;
}// size of (int) = 2 bytes
```

A. 2 n+8 **B.** 2 n+4 **C.** 2 n+2 **D.** 2 n

Q.2 What will be the output of the following pseudo-code?
For input a = 8 & b = 9.

```
function (input a, input b)
If (a< b)
return function (b, a)
elseif (b != 0)
return (a + function (a, b - 1))
else
return 0
```

A. 56 **B.** 88 **C.** 72 **D.** 65

Q.3 What will be the output of the following pseudo code?

```
Input m = 9, n = 6 ,
m = m + 1 ;
N = n - 1 ;
m = m + n
if (m >n)
print m
else
print n
```

A. 6 **B.** 5 **C.** 10 **D.** 15

Q.4 What will be the output of the following pseudo code?

```
Input f = 6, g = 9 and set sum = 0
Integer n if (g >f)
for (n = f; n< g; n = n + 1)
sum = sum + n
End for loop
else
print error message
print sum
```

A. 21 **B.** 15 **C.** 9 **D.** 6

Q.5 Consider a hash table with 9 slots. The hash function is h(k) = k mod 9. The collisions are resolved by chaining. The following 9 keys are inserted in the order: 5, 28, 19, 15, 20, 33, 12, 17, 10. The maximum, minimum, and average chain lengths in the hash table, respectively, are-

A. 3, 0, and 1 **B.** 3, 3, and 3
C. 4, 0, and 1 **D.** 3, 0, and 2

Q.6 How many instances of a class can be declared?

A. 1 **B.** 10
C. As per required **D.** None of the these

Q.7 What will the result of num variable after execution of the following statements?

```
int num = 58;
num % = 11;
```

A. 3 **B.** 5 **C.** 8 **D.** 11

Q.8 Predict the output of following python programs:

```
a = True
b = False
c = False
if not a or b:
print (1)
elif not a or not b and c:
print (2)
elif not a or b or not b and a:
print (3)
else:
print (4)
```

A. 1 **B.** 2 **C.** 3 **D.** 4

Q.9 C++ is a ______ type of language.

A. High-level Language
B. Low-level language
C. Middle-level language
D. None of the above

Q.10 For inserting a new line in the C++ program, which one of the following statements can be used?

A. \n **B.** \r
C. \a **D.** None of the above

Q.11 Which one of the following represents the tab?

A. \n **B.** \t
C. \r **D.** None of the above

Q.12 Predict the output of following python programs:

```
r = lambda q: q * 2
s = lambda q: q * 3
x = 2
x = r(x)
x = s(x)
x = r(x)
print (x)
```

A. 23 **B.** 7 **C.** 12 **D.** 24

Q.13 ____ is used to find and fix bugs in Java programs.

A. JVM **B.** JRE **C.** JDK **D.** JDB

Q.14 Which of the following is a valid long literal?

A. ABH8097 **B.** L990023
C. 904423 **D.** 0xnf029L

Q.15 What does the expression float a = 35 / 0 return?

A. 0 **B.** Not a Number
C. Infinity **D.** Run time exception

Q.16 Which among the following feature does not come under the concept of OOPS?

A. Data binding
B. Data hiding
C. Platform independent
D. Message passing

Q.17 We can create ____________ to an abstract class.

A. Pointers
B. References
C. Pointers or references
D. Can't create any reference, pointer or instance

Q.18 Which header file is required by the C++ programming language to use the OOPS concept?

A. stdio.h
B. iostream.h
C. stdlib.h
D. No need of header file

Q.19 Use of pointers or reference to an abstract class gives rise to which among the following feature?

A. Static Polymorphism
B. Runtime polymorphism
C. Compile-time Polymorphism
D. Polymorphism within methods

Q.20 Which of the following is not an OOPS concept?

A. Encapsulation **B.** Polymorphism
C. Exception **D.** Abstraction

Q.21 DNS can obtain the _________ of host if its domain name is known and vice versa.

A. Station address **B.** IP address
C. Port address **D.** Checksum

Q.22 A network, which is used for sharing data, software and hardware among several users of microcomputers, is called-

A. Wide Area Network.
B. Metropolitan Area Network.
C. Local Area Network.
D. Value Added Network.

Q.23 A VLAN equals to ________.

A. Router **B.** Subnet
C. Firewall **D.** Host/Client ID

Q.24 An example of a medium speed, switched communications service is:

A. Series 1000 **B.** Data phone 50
C. DDD **D.** None of these

Q.25 In the TCP/IP protocol suite, which of the following is an application layer protocol?

A. The User Datagram Protocol (UDP)
B. The Internet Protocol (IP)
C. The File Transfer Protocol (FTP)
D. The Transmission Control Protocol (TCP)

Q.26 In a relation database, every tuples divided into the fields are known as the _____.

A. Queries **B.** Domains
C. Relations **D.** Commit

Q.27 Which of the following keys is generally used to represents the relationships between the tables?

A. Primary key **B.** Foreign key
C. Secondary key **D.** None of the above

Q.28 In the relational table, which of the following can also be represented by the term "attribute"?

A. Entity **B.** Row **C.** Column **D.** Degree

Q.29 In the relational model, the relation are generally termed as ________.

A. Tuples **B.** Attributes
C. Rows **D.** Tables

Q.30 If a multivalued dependency holds and is not implied by the corresponding functional dependency, it usually arises from one of the following sources-

A. A many-to-many relationship set
B. A multivalued attribute of an entity set
C. A one-to-many relationship set
D. Both A many-to-many relationship set and A multivalued attribute of an entity set

Q.31 Which one of the following keyword is used to find out the number of values in a column?

A. TOTAL **B.** COUNT **C.** SUM **D.** ADD

Q.32 Which data type can store unstructured data in a column?

A. CHAR **B.** RAW
C. NUMERIC **D.** VARCHAR

Q.33 Which of the following is not Constraint in SQL?

A. Primary Key **B.** Not Null
C. Check **D.** Union

Q.34 A partitioned data set is most used for __________.

A. a program or source library
B. storing program data
C. storing backup information
D. storing ISAM files

Q.35 What is Page-map table?

A. It is a data file.
B. It is a directory.
C. It is used for address translation.
D. None of the above

Q.36 Which of the following HTML tag is used to display the text with scrolling effect?

A. <marquee> **B.** <scroll>
C. <div> **D.** None of the above

Q.37 Which of the following HTML tag is the special formatting tag?

A. <p> **B.** <b>
C. <pre> **D.** None of the above

Q.38 Which of the following is the container for <tr>, <th>, and <td> ?

A. <data>
B. <table>
C. <group>
D. All of the above

Q.39 In the maintenance phase the product must be tested against previous test cases. This is known as _________ testing.

A. Unit
B. Regression
C. Acceptance
D. Integration

Q.40 What is the major drawback of the Spiral Model?

A. Higher amount of risk analysis
B. Doesn't work well for smaller projects
C. Additional functionalities are added later on
D. Strong approval and documentation control

// Smart Answer Sheet //

Correct Indicates percentage of students who answered questions correctly.

Skipped Indicates percentage of students who skipped questions.

Q.	Ans.	Correct	Skipped
1	A	41.64 %	1.37 %
2	C	45.84 %	1.15 %
3	D	83.44 %	0.0 %
4	A	41.26 %	1.6 %
5	A	64.44 %	1.52 %
6	C	58.82 %	1.04 %
7	A	81.33 %	0.0 %
8	C	64.83 %	1.01 %
9	C	83.31 %	0.0 %
10	A	78.7 %	0.0 %
11	B	85.47 %	0.0 %
12	D	50.62 %	1.95 %
13	D	80.17 %	0.0 %
14	D	44.25 %	1.76 %
15	C	78.29 %	0.0 %
16	C	55.81 %	1.29 %
17	C	66.1 %	1.86 %
18	D	57.18 %	1.39 %
19	B	55.87 %	1.49 %
20	C	50.19 %	1.32 %
21	B	47.98 %	1.39 %
22	C	45.37 %	1.5 %
23	B	76.15 %	0.0 %
24	C	40.3 %	1.42 %
25	C	50.86 %	1.86 %
26	B	48.04 %	1.82 %
27	B	63.86 %	1.05 %
28	C	69.36 %	1.57 %
29	D	59.84 %	1.7 %
30	D	59.14 %	1.2 %
31	B	58.62 %	1.78 %
32	B	49.04 %	1.61 %
33	D	65.59 %	1.34 %
34	A	64.47 %	1.19 %
35	C	59.65 %	1.17 %
36	A	83.74 %	0.0 %
37	C	84.09 %	0.0 %
38	B	89.49 %	0.0 %
39	B	52.35 %	1.56 %
40	D	42.5 %	1.37 %

Performance Analysis	
Avg. Score (%)	60.0%
Toppers Score (%)	60.0%
Your Score	

//Hints and Solutions//

1. The code will acquire a space of 2n+8.

There are n elements in the array and the int data type acquires 2 bytes, so there will be 2n bytes acquired.

The int array occupies 4 bytes.

The sum variable will occupy 2 bytes.

The i variable will occupy 2 bytes.

So, total=2n+4+2+2=2n+8 bytes.

Hence, the correct option is (A).

2. function(8,9) will return function(9,8)

function(9,8) will return 9+function(9,7)

function(9,7) will return 9+9+function(9,6)

function(9,6) will return 9+9+9+function(9,5)

function(9,5) will return 9+9+9+9+function(9,4)

function(9,4) will return 9+9+9+9+9+function(9,3)

function(9,3) will return 9+9+9+9+9+9+function(9,2)

function(9,2) will return 9+9+9+9+9+9+9+function(9,1)

function(9,1) will return 9+9+9+9+9+9+9+9+function(9,0)

So the result is 72.

Hence, the correct option is (C).

3. m=10

N=5

m = m +n = 15

So, the output is 15.

Hence, the correct option is (D).

4. In this pseudo code, the for loop operates from n = 6 until n < 9.

In the first iteration we have the value of n = 6, s = 0 + 6 = 6.

In the next iteration we have the value of n = 7, s = 6 + 7 = 13.

In the third iteration we have the value of n = 8, s = 13 + 8 = 21.

The next iteration wouldn't be executed since the condition of the loop n < 9 becomes false. And thus the loop terminates.

So, the final answer we get is 21.

Hence, the correct option is (A).

5. Following are values of hash function for all keys
5 -->5
28 -->1
19 -->1 [Chained with 28]
15 -->6
20 -->2
33 -->6 [Chained with 15]
12 -->3
17 -->8
10 -->1 [Chained with 28 and 19]
The maximum chain length is 3.

The keys 28, 19 and 10 go to same slot 1, and form a chain of length 3.
The minimum chain length 0, there are empty slots (0, 4 and 7).
Average chain length is (0 + 3 + 1 + 1 + 0 + 1 + 2 + 0 + 1)/9 = 1.

Hence, the correct option is (A).

6. You can always declare multiple instances of a class, as per required. Each object will hold its own individual inner variables (unless they are static, in which case they are shared). An object is an instance of a class, and may be called a class instance or class object; instantiation is then also known as construction. Not all classes can be instantiated – abstract classes cannot be instantiated, while classes that can be instantiated are called concrete classes.

Hence, the correct option is (C).

7. num = 58
num % = 11
num = num % 11
num = 58 % 11
num = 3
There % represent remainder.

Hence, the correct option is (A).

8. In Python the precedence order is first NOT then AND and in last OR. So the if condition and second elif condition evaluates to False while third elif condition is evaluated to be True resulting in 3 as output.

Hence, the correct option is (C).

9. C++ is regarded as a middle-level language, as it comprises a combination of both high-level and low-level language features. It is a superset of C, and that virtually any legal C program is a legal C++ program. C++ runs on a variety of platforms, such as Windows, Mac OS, and the various versions of UNIX.

Hence, the correct option is (C).

10. To insert a new line or to jump on to the next line, one can use the "\n." In c++, there is also an alternative is available that is " endl," which is also used for breaking a line in the output. Let see the example of both the "\n" and "endl."

Example: Using "\n."

```
#include<iostream>

using namespace std;
int main() {
cout<< "Hello World! \n\n";
cout<< "I am learning C++";
return 0;
}
```

Output

Hello World!

I am learning C++

Hence, the correct option is (A).

11. The "\t" is a type of space sequence representing the tab, which means a set of blank space adds to the line. To understand it more clearly, consider the following example:

Program

```
#include<iostream>

using namespace std;
int main()
{
int a,b;
cout<<"Enter the first number\t";
cin>>a;
cout<<"Enter the second number\t";
cin>>b;
if(a>b)
cout<<"Greatest number is\t"<<a;

else
cout<<"Greatest number is\t"<<b;

<return 0;
}
```

Output

Enter the first number 12
Enter the second number 13
Greatest number is 13

Hence, the correct option is (B).

12. In the above program r and s are lambda functions or anonymous functions and q is the argument to both of the functions. In first step we have initialized x to 2. In second step we have passed x as argument to the lambda function r, this will return x*2 which is stored in x. That is, x = 4 now. Similarly in third step we have passed x to lambda function s, So x = 4*3. i.e, x = 12 now. Again in the last step, x is multiplied by 2 by passing it to function r. Therefore, x = 24.

Hence, the correct option is (D).

13. JDB (Java Debugger) is a command-line java debugger that debugs the java class. It is a part of the Java Platform Debugger Architecture (JPDA) that helps in the inspections and debugging of a local or remote Java Virtual Machine (JVM).

The JVM (Java Virtual Machine) enables a computer to run Java or other language (kotlin, groovy, Scala, etc.) programs that are compiled to the Java bytecode. The JRE (Java Runtime Environment) is a part of JDK that contains the Java class libraries, Java class loader, and the Java Virtual Machine. The JDK (Java Development Kit) is a software development environment used to develop Java applications and applets.

Hence, the correct option is (D).

14. For every long literal to be recognized by Java, we need to add L character at the end of the expression. It can be either uppercase (L) or lowercase (l) character. However, it is recommended to use uppercase character instead of lowercase because the lowercase (l) character is hard to distinguish from the uppercase (i) character.

For example,

1. Lowercase l: 0x466rffl
2. Uppercase L: 0nhf450L

Hence, the correct option is (D).

15. In Java, whenever we divide any number (double, float, and long except integer) by zero, it results in infinity. According to the IEEE Standard for Floating-Point Arithmetic (IEEE 754), if we divide 1/0 will give positive infinity, -1/0 will give negative infinity, and 0/0 will give NaN. But on dividing an integer by zero, it throws a runtime exception, i.e., java.lang.ArithmeticException.

Hence, the correct option is (C).

16. Platform independence is a feature that does not come under the OOPS concepts. This feature depends on the programming language. C++ is an object-oriented programming language that is not a platform-independent language.

Hence, the correct option is (C).

17. Abstract classes act as expressions of general concepts from which more specific classes can be derived. You can't create an object of an abstract class type. However, you can use pointers and references to abstract class types. You create an abstract class by declaring at least one pure virtual member function.

Hence, the correct option is (C).

18. We can easily use the OOPS concepts in C++ programs without using any header file. There is no need to use any particular header file for using the OOPS concept in the C++ programs. The C++ functions and variables have their respective header files, which should be defined in the program. The main aim of OOP is to bind together the data and the functions that operate on them so that no other part of the code can access this data except that function.

Hence, the correct option is (D).

19. The runtime polymorphism is supported by reference and pointer to an abstract class. This relies upon a base class pointer and reference to select the proper virtual function. Runtime polymorphism is a process in which a call to an overridden method is resolved at runtime rather than compile-time. In this process, an overridden method is called through the reference variable of a superclass.

Hence, the correct option is (B).

20. The exception is not an OOPS concept. An exception is an event, which occurs during the execution of a program, that disrupts the normal flow of the program's instructions. When an error occurs within a method, the method creates an object and hands it off to the runtime system.

OOPs concept have:

- Object
- Class
- Inheritance
- Polymorphism
- Abstraction
- Encapsulation

Hence, the correct option is (C).

21. DNS can obtain the IP address of the host if its domain name is known and vice versa. DNS automatically converts between the names we type in our Web browser address bar to the IP addresses of Web servers hosting.

Hence, the correct option is (B).

22. A local area network is a group of computers and associated devices that share a common communications line or wireless link to a server. A local area network is a computer network that interconnects computers within a limited area such as a residence, school, laboratory, university campus or office building.

Hence, the correct option is (C).

23. VLAN and Subnet are both developed to deal with segmenting or partitioning a portion of the network. And they also share such similarities as restricting broadcast domains or ensuring security through isolation of different sub-networks.

Hence, the correct option is (B).

24. DDD (domain-driven design) approach enables the development of software that is focused on the complex requirements of those that need it and doesn't waste effort on anything unneeded. The clients of domain-driven design are often enterprise-level businesses.

Hence, the correct option is (C).

25. The File Transfer Protocol (FTP) is an application layer protocol. File transfer protocol is a way to download, upload, and transfer files from one location to another on the internet and between computer systems. FTP enables the transfer of files back and forth between computers or through the cloud. Users require an internet connection in order to execute FTP transfers.

Hence, the correct option is (C).

26. In a relation database, the number of rows inside a table is known as tuples, and if we further divide those tuples (or rows) into those fields, they become the domains. A domain is a unique set of values permitted for an attribute in a table.

Hence, the correct option is (B).

27. To represent the relationships between the various tables in the database, generally, the foreign key is used. A foreign key is a column or group of columns in a relational database table that provides a link between data in two tables. It acts as a cross-reference between tables because it references the primary key of another table, thereby establishing a link between them.

Hence, the correct option is (B).

28. In the relational database, the number of rows inside a table is called the tuples, and the numbers of columns are known as the attributes. attributes are the describing characteristics or properties that define all items pertaining to a certain category applied to all cells of a column.

Hence, the correct option is (C).

29. In the relation model, the relations are also referred to as the tables because the relations are considered as the technical name of the table. Tables are database objects that contain all the data in a database. In tables, data is logically organized in a row-and-column format similar to a spreadsheet. Each row represents a unique record, and each column represents a field in the record.

Hence, the correct option is (D).

30. For a many-to-many relationship set each related entity set has its own schema and there is an additional schema for the relationship set. For a multivalued attribute, a separate schema is created consisting of that attribute and the primary key of the entity set.

Hence, the correct option is (D).

31. The "COUNT" keyword is used to find the total number of values inside a column. So whenever a user wants to find the total values in a column, he can use the keyword "COUNT".

Example:

```
SELECT COUNT (expression)
FROM tables
WHERE conditions;
```

Hence, the correct option is (B).

32. RAW datatype stores variable-length binary data that can be queried and inserted but not manipulated. Its maximum length is 32767 bytes.

CHAR stores character data in a fixed length.

NUMERIC stores numeric values only.

VARCHAR stores variable string data in a fixed length. Its maximum length is 4000 bytes.

Hence, the correct option is (B).

33. Constraint specifies the rule to allow or restrict what data will be stored in a table. The Primary Key, Not Null, and Check are the constraints that specify rules for data insertion.

Union is an operator that combines two or more results from multiple select queries into a single result set.

Hence, the correct option is (D).

34. A partitioned data set is most used for a program or source library. A partitioned data set (PDS) is a data set containing multiple members, each of which holds a separate sub-data set, similar to a directory in other types of file systems.

Hence, the correct option is (A).

35. Page-map table is used for address translation. A page table is the data structure used by a virtual memory system in a computer operating system to store the mapping between virtual addresses and physical addresses. Virtual addresses are used by the program executed by the accessing process, while physical addresses are used by the hardware, or more specifically, by the RAM subsystem. The page table is a key component of virtual address translation which is necessary to access data in memory.

Hence, the correct option is (C).

36. The <marquee> tag is a non-standard HTML element that is used to scroll a text or image either horizontally or vertically. In simple words, we can say that it automatically scrolls the image or text in up, down, left, and right direction.

Example:

```
<marquee>
  <--- contents --->
</marquee>
```

Hence, the correct option is (A).

37. The HTML <pre> tag is used to specify pre-formatted texts. Texts within <pre>...</pre> tag is displayed in a fixed-width font. Usually, it is displayed in courier font. It maintains both line break space.

Syntax:

```
<pre> Contents... </pre>
```

Hence, the correct option is (C).

38. The <table> tag in HTML, is generally used to display data in tabular format. We can create a table to display the data in the tabular form using the <table> element, with the help of <tr>, <th>, and <td> elements.

Example:

```
<table border="1">
 <tr>
  <th>Month</th>
  <th>Savings</th>
 </tr>
 <tr>
  <td>January</td>
  <td>$100</td>
 </tr>
</table>
```

Hence, the correct option is (B).

39. In the maintenance phase the product must be tested against previous test cases. This is known as Regression testing. Regression testing is a testing that is done to confirm that a code change in the software does not affect the existing functionality of the product. This test can be executed on the latest build when there is a critical change in the original functionality that too even in a solitary bug fix.

Hence, the correct option is (B).

40. A spiral model is an incremental approach, which is formed as a combination of the waterfall model and prototyping model. The major drawbacks of the Spiral model are as follows:

- Expensive
- Doesn't work well for smaller projects
- Risk analysis requires highly skilled experts.

Hence, the correct option is (D).

Mock Test 05

Q.1 What is the output?

```
a += 2;
b += 1;
}
int main()
{
int x = 10, y = 2;
fun(x, y);
cout<< x<< " "<< y<< " ";
fun(x, y);
cout<< x<< " "<< y;
```

A. 10 2 10 2 **B.** 12 2 14 2
C. 12 3 14 3 **D.** 12 2 14 3

Q.2 What is the output?

```
int a = 100;
printf("%0 %x", a);
```

A. %a **B.** %x **C.** 100 **D.** None

Q.3 What is the output?

```
typedef int num;
num bunk = 0.00;
printf("%d", bunk);
```

A. 0 **B.** 0.0
C. Garbage value **D.** Logical Error

Q.4 What is the output-

```
float x = 0.0;
long int y = 10;
printf("%d", sizeof(y) == sizeof(x+y));
```

A. 1 **B.** 0 **C.** 4 **D.** 8

Q.5 What Is The Output Of this program?

```
void f2(int p = 30)
{
for (int i = 20; i<= p; i += 5)
cout<< i<< " ";
}
void f1(int& m)
{
m += 10;
f2(m);
}
int main()
{
int n = 20;
f1(n);
cout<< n<< " ";
return 0;
}
```

A. 25 30 35 20 **B.** 20 25 30 20
C. 25 30 25 30 **D.** 20 25 30 30

Q.6 Which of the following SLT template class is a container adaptor class?

A. Stack **B.** List **C.** Deque **D.** Vector

Q.7 Predict the output of following python programs:

```
count = 1
def doThis():
global count
for i in (1, 2, 3):
count += 1
doThis()
print (count)
```

A. 1 **B.** 2 **C.** 3 **D.** 4

Q.8 Let p1 be an integer pointer with a current value of 2000. What is the content of p1 after the expression p1++ has been evaluated?

A. 2001 **B.** 2002 **C.** 2004 **D.** 2008

Q.9 Which of the following refers to characteristics of an array?

A. An array is a set of similar data items
B. An array is a set of distinct data items
C. An array can hold different types of datatypes
D. None of the above

Q.10 Predict the output of following Python Programs.

```
class Acc:
def __init__(self, id):
self.id = id
id = 555
acc = Acc(111)
print acc.id
```

A. 555 **B.** 111 **C.** 5 **D.** 1

Q.11 Which of the following is the correct syntax for declaring the array?

A. init array [] **B.** int array [5];
C. Array[5]; **D.** None of the above

Q.12 Which of the following statement is not true about C++?

A. Members of a class are public by default
B. A class cannot have the private members
C. A structure can have the member functions
D. All of the above

Q.13 Evaluate the following Java expression, if x=3, y=5, and z=10:

++z + y - y + z + x++

A. 24 **B.** 23 **C.** 20 **D.** 25

Q.14 What will be the output of the following program?

```
public class Test {
public static void main(String[] args) {
int count = 1;
while (count<= 15) {
```

```
System.out.println(count % 2 == 1 ? "***" : "+++++");
++count;
} // end while
} // end main
}
```

A. 15 times ***
B. 15 times +++++
C. 8 times *** and 7 times +++++
D. Both will print only once

Q.15 Which of the following tool is used to generate API documentation in HTML format from doc comments in source code?

A. javap tool **B.** javaw command
C. Javadoc tool **D.** javah command

Q.16 Which among the following best describes the Inheritance?

A. Copying the code already written.
B. Using the code already written once.
C. Using already defined functions in programming language.
D. Using the data and functions into derived segment.

Q.17 Which function best describe the concept of polymorphism in programming languages?

A. Class member function
B. Virtual function
C. Inline function
D. Undefined function

Q.18 Which among the following best defines single level inheritance?

A. A class inheriting a derived class.
B. A class inheriting a base class.
C. A class inheriting a nested class.
D. A class which gets inherited by 2 classes.

Q.19 Which feature of OOPS described the reusability of code?

A. Abstraction **B.** Encapsulation
C. Polymorphism **D.** Inheritance

Q.20 Which programming language doesn't support multiple inheritance?

A. C++ and Java **B.** C and C++
C. Java and SmallTalk **D.** Java

Q.21 The Sharing of a medium and its path by two or more devices is called-

A. Modulation **B.** Encoding
C. Multiplexing **D.** Line discipline

Q.22 Which of the following statements is true?

A. TCP / IP Model developed before OSI model.
B. TCP / IP model developed after the OSI model.
C. TCP / IP model developed simaltaneousaly to the Model OSI model.
D. TCP / IP model developed to overcome the shortcomings of OSI Model.

Q.23 What is the use of FTP?

A. To view a file on a remote computer.
B. To identify the name of the domain.
C. To identify the name of the host.
D. To send the file to the network.

Q.24 Which of the following algorithms is not used in asymmetric-key cryptography?

A. RSA algorithm
B. Diffie-Hellman algorithm
C. Electronic code book algorithm
D. None of the mentioned

Q.25 How many TCP connections does FTP use?

A. One **B.** Two **C.** Three **D.** Four

Q.26 The Database Management Query language is generally designed for the __________.

A. Support end-users who use English like commands
B. Specifying the structure of the database
C. Support in the development of the complex applications software
D. All of the above

Q.27 An _______ is a set of entities of the same type that share the same properties, or attributes.

A. Entity set **B.** Attribute set
C. Relation set **D.** Entity model

Q.28 Which of the following levels is considered as the level closed to the end-users?

A. Internal Level **B.** External Level
C. Conceptual Level **D.** Physical Level

Q.29 A computer security protocol for logging in can be considered as the example of the _____ component of an information system.

A. Data **B.** Software
C. Procedure **D.** Hardware

Q.30 The descriptive property possessed by each entity set is ________.

A. Entity **B.** Attribute **C.** Relation **D.** Model

Q.31 Which of the following is not a valid aggregate function?

A. COUNT **B.** COMPUTE
C. SUM **D.** MAX

Q.32 Which data manipulation command is used to combines the records from one or more tables?

A. SELECT **B.** PROJECT
C. JOIN **D.** PRODUCT

Q.33 Which operator is used to compare a value to a specified list of values?

A. ANY **B.** BETWEEN
C. ALL **D.** IN

Q.34 Which program runs first after booting the computer and loading the GUI?

A. Desktop Manager **B.** File Manager
C. Windows Explorer **D.** Authentication

Q.35 Which of the following is an example of a Real Time Operating System?

A. MAC
B. MS-DOS
C. Windows 10
D. Process Control

Q.36 What are the types of unordered or bulleted list in HTML?

A. Disc, square, triangle
B. Polygon, triangle, circle
C. Disc, circle, square
D. All of the above

Q.37 Which of the following HTML attribute is used to define inline styles?

A. Style
B. Type
C. Class
D. None of the above

Q.38 Which of the following is the paragraph tag in HTML?

A. <p>
B. <b>
C. <pre>
D. None of the above

Q.39 Most of the effort in Classical waterfall model is required in:

A. Design phase
B. Development phase
C. Maintenance Phase
D. Testing Phase

Q.40 What is the major drawback of using RAD Model?

A. Highly specialized & skilled developers/designers are required.
B. Increases reusability of components.
C. Encourages customer/client feedback.
D. Increases reusability of components, Highly specialized & skilled developers/designers are required.

// Smart Answer Sheet //

Correct Indicates percentage of students who answered questions correctly.

Skipped Indicates percentage of students who skipped questions.

Q.	Ans.	Correct	Skipped
1	B	54.41 %	1.78 %
2	B	89.45 %	0.0 %
3	A	66.29 %	1.17 %
4	B	43.19 %	1.33 %
5	D	69.52 %	1.87 %
6	A	54.14 %	1.88 %
7	D	59.56 %	1.76 %
8	C	89.45 %	0.0 %
9	A	80.72 %	0.0 %
10	B	57.44 %	1.86 %
11	B	58.61 %	1.96 %
12	C	77.65 %	0.0 %
13	D	83.14 %	0.0 %
14	C	67.22 %	1.17 %
15	C	68.82 %	1.78 %
16	D	52.9 %	1.64 %
17	B	51.28 %	1.03 %
18	B	59.8 %	1.71 %
19	D	58.77 %	1.21 %
20	D	80.89 %	0.0 %
21	C	42.54 %	1.31 %
22	A	12.74 %	4.73 %
23	D	61.46 %	1.82 %
24	C	78.03 %	0.0 %
25	B	56.04 %	1.79 %
26	D	20.07 %	3.49 %
27	A	66.83 %	1.26 %
28	B	50.13 %	1.99 %
29	C	64.84 %	1.33 %
30	B	54.68 %	1.56 %
31	B	85.0 %	0.0 %
32	C	65.27 %	1.82 %
33	D	48.72 %	1.81 %
34	D	62.08 %	1.78 %
35	D	55.99 %	1.41 %
36	C	82.42 %	0.0 %
37	A	89.05 %	0.0 %
38	A	77.13 %	0.0 %
39	C	60.52 %	1.89 %
40	D	40.18 %	1.64 %

Performance Analysis	
Avg. Score (%)	62.5%
Toppers Score (%)	70.0%
Your Score	

//Hints and Solutions//

1. In the above program, in main() we pass two values x or y in fun() and fun() received the reference of x so, increment it's value but y have incremented but not a reference so, y is same in main block. Therefore, the output is 12 2 14 2.

Hence, the correct option is (B).

2. In this question %0 will cancel out the a while %x will get printed, but, if we only write printf("%x"); without passing any parameter for x.
It will show an error.

So, the output is %x.

Hence, the correct option is (B).

3. Integer part of 0.00 is equal to 0.

So, only 0 will be printed with printf("%d", bunk) when 0.00 is passed.

Because %d stands for integer.

Hence, the correct option is (A).

4. sizeof(x) that is float is 4.

sizeof(y) that is long int is 8.

sizeof(x+y) that also comes out to be float will have size = 4=

here, it is asking sizeof(y) ==sizeof(x+y)

i.e, 8 == 4

"==" operator gives result in either 0 or 1.

So, output is 0.

Hence, the correct option is (B).

5. In this program, main() call the f1() and pass the value of n in f1() and f1() is received the reference of n and increments 10 of it's value now n is 30. Again call f2() and pass the value of m in f2(), f2() receive the value of m and check the condition and print the value. Therefore, the output is 20 25 30 30.

Hence, the correct option is (D).

6. The STL provides three container adapters stack, queue and priority queue. Adapters are not first-class containers, because they do not provide the actual data-structure implementation in which elements can be stored and because adapters do not support iterators. The benefit of an adapter class is that the programmer can choose an appropriate underlying data structure. All three adapter classes provide member functions push and pop that properly insert an element into each adapter data structure and properly remove an element from each adapter data structure. STL is stands for Standard Template Library.

Hence, the correct option is (A).

7. The variable count declared outside the function is global variable and also the count variable being referenced in the function is the same global variable defined outside of the function. So, the changes made to variable in the function is reflected to the original variable. So, the output of the program is 4.

Hence, the correct option is (D).

8. The size of one pointer integer is 4 bytes. The current value of p1 is 2000.

p1++ = p1 + 1

p1++ = 2000 + 4 = 2004

Hence, the correct option is (C).

9. An array is a data structure that contains a group of elements. Typically these elements are all of the same data type, such as an integer or string. Arrays are commonly used in computer programs to organize data so that a related set of values can be easily sorted or searched.

Hence, the correct option is (A).

10. Instantiation of the class "Acc" automatically calls the method __init__ and passes the object as the self parameter. 111 is assigned to data attribute of the object called id.

The value "555" is not retained in the object as it is not assigned to a data attribute of the class/object. So, the output of the program is "111".

Hence, the correct option is (B).

11. To declare an array in C++, we first need to specify its data type according to requirements such as int or char, afterward that the array's name and the size of the array.

Example: Array declaration by specifying size and initializing elements.

int arr[8] = { 10, 20, 30, 40 };

The compiler will create an array of size 8, initializes the first four elements as specified by the user and rest elements as 0.

Hence, the correct option is (B).

12. In C, structures are not allowed to have member functions; while on the other hand, C++ allows the structure to have the member functions. Members of the class are generally private by default, and those of the structures are public. So it is a completely false statement that classes can not private members.

Hence, the correct option is (C).

13. In the above expression, ++z means that the value will first increment by 1, i.e. 11. So, the value z is 11. Now, evaluate the statement by putting the values of x, y, and z. On evaluating the expression, we get

++z +y -y +z + x++

11 + 5 - 5 + 11 + 3 = 25

Here, x++=3, because that is postfix increment which is increase after execution.

Hence, the correct option is (D).

14. In the above code, we have declared count = 1. The value of count will be increased till 14 because of the while (count<=15)

statement. If the remainder is equal to 1 on dividing the count by 2, it will print (***) else print (+++++). Therefore, for all odd numbers till 15 (1, 3, 5, 7, 9, 11, 13, 15), it will print (***), and for all even numbers till 14 (2, 4, 6, 8, 10, 12, 14) it will print (+++++).

Therefore, an asterisk (***) will be printed eight times, and plus (+++++) will be printed seven times.

Hence, the correct option is (C).

15. The Javadoc is a tool that is used to generate API documentation in HTML format from the Java source files. In other words, it is a program (tool) that reads a collection of source files into an internal form.

The Javadoc command line syntax is,

Javadoc [options] [packagenames] [sourcefiles] [@files].

The javap tool is used to get the information of any class or interface. It is also known as a disassembler. The javaw command is identical to java that displays a window with error information, and the javah command is used to generate native method functions.

Hence, the correct option is (C).

16. Inheritance can only be indicated by using the data and functions that we use in derived class, being provided by parent class. Copying code is nowhere similar to this concept, also using the code already written is same as copying. Using already defined functions is not inheritance as we are not adding any of our own features.

Hence, the correct option is (D).

17. Virtual function best describes the concept of polymorphism in programming languages. Only those functions are used to achieve the polymorphism, which is declared as 'virtual'. These functions let the OOPS programs decide at runtime which function is to be called by the pointer.

Hence, the correct option is (B).

18. Single inheritance is one in which the derived class inherits the single base class either publicly, privately or protectedly. In single inheritance, the derived class uses the features or members of the single base class. These base class members can be accessed by derived class or child class according to the access specifier specified during inheriting the parent class or base class.

Hence, the correct option is (B).

19. Inheritance is the feature of OOPS, which allows the users of OOPS to reuse the code which is already written. This OOPS feature inherits the features of another class in the programs. This mechanism actually inherits the fields and methods of the superclass.

Hence, the correct option is (D).

20. Java doesn't support multiple inheritances. But that feature can be implemented by using the concept of the interface. Multiple inheritances is not supported because of the diamond problem and similar issues.

Hence, the correct option is (D).

21. Multiplexing is a method by which multiple analog or digital signals are combined into one signal over a shared medium. The multiplexed signal is transmitted over a communication channel such as a cable. Multiplexing divides the capacity of the communication channel into several logical changes.

Hence, the correct option is (C).

22. The TCP/IP model, which is realistically the Internet Model, came into existence about 10 years before the OSI model. The TCP/IP model is a concise version of the OSI model. It contains four layers, unlike seven layers in the OSI model. The layers are:

- Process/Application Layer
- Host-to-Host/Transport Layer
- Internet Layer
- Network Access/Link Layer

Hence, the correct option is (A).

23. FTP is used to transfer files between computers on a network. You can use FTP to exchange files between computer accounts, transfer files between an account and a desktop computer, or access online software archives.

Hence, the correct option is (D).

24. An electronic code book algorithm is a mode of operation for a block cipher, where each frame of text in an encrypted document refers to a data field. In other terms, the same plaintext value would also give the same value for ciphertext.

Hence, the correct option is (C).

25. FTP uses two TCP connections for communication. One to pass control information, and is not used to send files on port 21, only control information. And the other, a data connection on port 20 to send the data files between the client and the server.

Hence, the correct option is (B).

26. The database management query language is generally designed by keeping in mind that it must support the end-users who are familiar with the English-like commands. It should also boost the process of development of the complex applications software and helps in specifying the structure of the database.

Hence, the correct option is (D).

27. Entity Set is a collection or a group of 'entities' sharing exactly the 'same set of attributes'. All entities can be distinctly identified in an entity set. This is because all the entities have a different set of value for some set of attributes. We further classify the entity set into two basic categories Strong and Weak entity set. The collection of entity sets and their relationship sets together forms a database.

Hence, the correct option is (A).

28. The database's external level is the one and only level that is considered the closest level to the end-users. This is the highest level in the three level architecture and closest to the user. It is also known as the view level. The external level only shows the relevant database content to the users in the form of views and hides the rest of the data.

Hence, the correct option is (B).

29. A computer security protocol for logging in can be considered as the procedure component of an information system. Information system, an integrated set of components for collecting, storing, and processing data and for providing information, knowledge, and digital products.

Hence, the correct option is (C).

30. Attribute is descriptive properties possessed by all members of an entity set. Each entity has a value for each of its attributes. A subset of the attributes form a primary key of the entity-set; i.e., uniquely identifying each member of the set.

Hence, the correct option is (B).

31. Aggregate function is used to perform calculations on multiple values and return the output in a single value. It is mostly used with the SELECT statement. COUNT, SUM, and MAX are all aggregate functions.

COMPUTE is not an aggregate function. It is used to generate totals as an additional column at the end of the result set.

Hence, the correct option is (B).

32. JOIN command is used with the SELECT statement to retrieve data from multiple tables. It must be needed whenever we want to fetch records from two or more tables.

Syntax:

```
SELECT table1.column1,table1.column2,table2.column1,....
FROM table1
JOIN table2
ON table1.matching_column = table2.matching_column;
```

Hence, the correct option is (C).

33. The IN operator easily tests the expression if it matches any value in a specified list of values. It reduces the use of multiple OR conditions.

The WHERE or HAVING clause uses the ANY and ALL operators. ANY gives the result when any subquery value matches the specified condition. The ALL give the result when all subquery values match the specified condition.

The BETWEEN operator selects values only in the given range.

Hence, the correct option is (D).

34. The authentication program is run first after booting the computer and loading the GUI. Authentication is a process of verifying the person or device. For example, when you log in to Facebook, you enter a username and password.

Hence, the correct option is (D).

35. Process control is a best example of a Real time operating system. The function of the realtime operation system is to control resources in the system shared by application tasks including input/output devices, computer memory, and the CPU itself.

Hence, the correct option is (D).

36. The unordered or bulleted list in HTML is used to display the elements in a bulleted format. Mainly, there are three types of an unordered list: disc, circle, and square.

Disc: Sets the list item marker to a bullet i.e. default.

syntax:

```
<ul style="list-style-type:disc">
</ul>
```

Circle: Sets the list item marker to a circle.

syntax:

```
<ul style="list-style-type:circle">
</ul>
```

Square: Sets the list item marker to a square.

syntax:

```
<ul style="list-style-type:square">
</ul>
```

Hence, the correct option is (C).

37. The style attribute in HTML is used to change the style of existing HTML elements. It can be used with any HTML tag. To apply the style on the HTML tag, you should have the basic knowledge of CSS properties.

Hence, the correct option is (A).

38. The <p> (paragraph tag) tag in HTML is used to define a paragraph in a webpage. The HTML <p> tag indicates the starting of new paragraph.

Syntax:

```
<p> Content </p>
```

Hence, the correct option is (A).

39. Most of the effort in Classical waterfall model is required in maintenance Phase. On average around 60% of total effort is needed in Maintenance Phase. Around 20% is needed in testing and 7% in coding and 10% in Design and 3% in requirement analysis and specification.

Hence, the correct option is (C).

40. The major drawback of using RAD Model are:

- The use of powerful and efficient tools requires highly skilled professionals.
- The absence of reusable components can lead to failure of the project.
- The team leader must work closely with the developers and customers to close the project in time.
- The systems which cannot be modularized suitably cannot use this model.
- Customer involvement is required throughout the life cycle.

- It is not meant for small scale projects as for such cases, the cost of using automated tools and techniques may exceed the entire budget of the project.

Hence, the correct option is (D).

Mock Test 06

Q.1 What will be the output of the following pseudocode:

```
int go = 5.0, num = 1*10;
do
{
num /= go;
} while(go--);
printf ("%d\n", num);
```

A. Floating Poing Exception
B. Comlpilation Error
C. 3 6 7
D. None

Q.2 What will be the output of following pseudo code:

```
float x = 0.0;
long int y = 10;
printf("%d", sizeof(x) == sizeof(x+y));
```

A. 1 **B.** 0 **C.** 4 **D.** 8

Q.3 What will be the output of the following pseudocode:

```
int num = 987;
int rem;
while(num!=0)
{
rem = num % 4;
num = num / 10;
}
printf("%d",rem);
```

A. 0 **B.** 1 **C.** 2 **D.** 3

Q.4 What will be the output of the following Pseudo Code.

```
float i;
i = 1;
printf("%d",i);
```

A. 1 **B.** Garbage Value
C. 1.000000 **D.** Error

Q.5 What will be the output of the following pseudocode:

```
public class Main
{
public static void main(String[] args)
{
String names[] = new String[5];
for(int x=0; x<args.length; x++)
names[x] = args[x];
System.out.println(names[2]);
}
}
```

A. Name
B. Null
C. Compilation fails
D. An exception Throws at runtime

Q.6 If a = 0x6db7 and b = 0xa726, what will be the value of a^b?

A. 51956 **B.** 51256 **C.** 51857 **D.** 51235

Q.7 Study the following program:

```
main ()
{
int x;
x = 4 % -5 + 6 % 5;
printf("\nx = %d", x);
}
```

What will be the output of this program?

A. 10 **B.** 9 **C.** 5 **D.** 3

Q.8 How many types of variables are there in the C language?

A. 2 **B.** 4 **C.** 1 **D.** 5

Q.9 Which one of the following given statements is not true about the references in C++?

A. A reference should be initialized whenever it is declared.
B. A reference cannot refer to a constant value.
C. A reference cannot be NULL.
D. Once a reference is created, it cannot be later made to reference another object; it cannot be reset.

Q.10 Read the following given program of C++ and predict the most appropriate output of the following program?

```
#include<iostream>
using namespace std;
int&fun()
{
static int x = 10;
return x;
}
int main()
{
fun() = 30;
cout<< fun();
return 0;
}
```

A. It will obtain a compilation error
B. It will print 30 as output
C. It will print ten as output
D. None of the above

Q.11 Which of the following functions must use the reference?

A. Copy constructor
B. Destructor
C. Parameterized constructor
D. None of the above

Q.12 What do you mean by chained exception in Java?

A. Exceptions occurred by the VirtualMachineError.
B. An exception caused by other exceptions.
C. Exceptions occur in chains with discarding the debugging information.
D. None of the above

Q.13 In which memory a String is stored, when we create a string using new operator?

A. Stack
B. String memory
C. Heap memory
D. Random storage space

Q.14 Direction: Predict the output of following Python Programs.

```
for i in  range(2):
print i
for i in range(4,6):
print i
```

A.	B.	C.	D.
0	0	0	0
1	1	2	1
4	2	3	3
5	3	4	5

Q.15 Direction: Predict the output of following Python Programs.

```
values = [1, 2, 3, 4]
numbers = set(values)
def checknums(num):
if num in numbers:
return True
else:
return False
for i in filter(checknums, values):
print i
```

A. 1 **B.** 2 **C.** 3 **D.** 4

Q.16 The functions go in the ______ section of a class definition.

A. Declaration **B.** Implementation
C. Prototype **D.** Functioning

Q.17 Which of the following will increase the value stored in the first element of the fee array by 2 ?

A. amount[0]=amount[0]+2;
B. amount fee[0]=amount fee[0]+2;
C. feelnfo.amount[0]=feelnfo.amount fee[0]+2;
D. fee[0].amount=feel[0].amount+2;

Q.18 A ________ is a member function that is declared within a base class and redefined by a derived class.

A. Class member function
B. Virtual function
C. Inline function
D. Undefined function

Q.19 To use the this pointer with a member function, you _______.

A. Declare this as static.
B. Declare this as global.
C. Define this as equal to the address of the appropriate object.
D. Do nothing; it is automatically supplied for you.

Q.20 The C++ keyword for declaring a variable that contains a decimal point is _______.

A. Dec **B.** Decimal **C.** Float **D.** Floater

Q.21 Which one of the following is not a network topology?

A. Ring **B.** Star
C. Bus **D.** Peer to Peer

Q.22 The maximum length (in bytes) of an IPv4 datagram is:

A. 32 **B.** 1024 **C.** 65536 **D.** 512

Q.23 The term IANA stands for?

A. Internet Assigned Numbers Authority
B. Internal Assigned Numbers Authority
C. Internet Associative Numbers Authoritative
D. Internal Associative Numbers Authority

Q.24 How many digits of the Data Network Identification Code (DNIC) identify the country?

A. First three **B.** First four
C. First five **D.** First six

Q.25 MODEM word is made from:

A. Modulation, Demodulation
B. Modulation, Rough modulation
C. Modulation, Defination
D. (A) and (B) both

Q.26 Which one of the following statements about normal forms is FALSE?

A. BCNF is stricter than 3NF.
B. Lossless, dependency-preserving decomposition into 3NF is always possible.
C. Lossless, dependency-preserving decomposition into BCNF is always possible.
D. Any relation with two attributes is in BCNF.

Q.27 Which one of the following is a type of Data Manipulation Command?

A. Create **B.** Alter
C. Delete **D.** All of the above

Q.28 ___________ can help us detect poor E-R design.

A. Database Design Process
B. E-R Design Process
C. Relational scheme
D. Functional dependencies

Q.29 Which of the following functional dependencies hold for relations R(A, B, C) and S(B, D, E):

$B \rightarrow A$,

$A \rightarrow C$

The relation R contains 200 tuples and the rel ation S contains 100 tuples. What is the maximum number of tuples possible in the natural join R◊◊S (R natural join S)?

A. 100 **B.** 200 **C.** 300 **D.** 2000

Q.30 Which one of the following keywords are used to find out the number of values in a column?

A. TOTAL **B.** COUNT **C.** SUM **D.** ADD

Q.31 Which of the following statement is correct regarding the difference between TRUNCATE, DELETE and DROP command?

I. DELETE operation can be rolled back but TRUNCATE and DROP operations cannot be rolled back.

II. TRUNCATE and DROP operations can be rolled back but DELETE operations cannot be rolled back.

III. DELETE is an example of DML, but TRUNCATE and DROP are examples of DDL.

IV. All are an example of DDL.

A. I and III **B.** II and III **C.** II and IV **D.** II and IV

Q.32 Which of the following options are correct regarding these three keys (Primary Key, Super Key, and Candidate Key) in a database?

I. Minimal super key is a candidate key.

II. Only one candidate key can be a primary key.

III. All super keys can be a candidate key.

IV. We cannot find a primary key from the candidate key.

A. I and II **B.** II and III **C.** I and III **D.** II and IV

Q.33 In MS-DOS, relocatable object files and load modules have extensions:

A. .OBJ and .COM or .EXE, respectively

B. .COM and .OBJ, respectively

C. .EXE and .OBJ, respectively

D. .DAS and .EXE, respectively

Q.34 The state transition initiated by the user process itself in an operating system is:

A. Block **B.** Dispatch

C. Wake up **D.** Timer run out

Q.35 What does wrap attribute denote?

A. Whether the text is in bold

B. Whether the text is wrapped

C. Whether the text is in italics

D. Whether the text is highlighted

Q.36 Which of the following defines a default value on page load?

A. <object> **B.** <input>

C. <progress> **D.** <area>

Q.37 How title attribute works?

A. Specifies extra information about an element.

B. Focus text when hovering over the element.

C. Highlight text when hovering over the element.

D. Zoom in and zoom out text when hovering over the element.

Q.38 In iterative waterfall model the error committed during which phase cannot be corrected?

A. Requirement gathering

B. Feasibility study

C. Requirement analysis

D. Coding

Q.39 Before actual software development begins, this model requires to build the toy implementation of it.

A. Iterative waterfall model

B. RAD model

C. Agile model

D. Prototype model

Q.40 When the wildcard in a WHERE clause is useful?

A. When an exact match is required in a SELECT statement.

B. When an exact match is not possible in a SELECT statement.

C. When an exact match is required in a CREATE statement.

D. When an exact match is not possible in a CREATE statement.

// Smart Answer Sheet //

Correct Indicates percentage of students who answered questions correctly.

Skipped Indicates percentage of students who skipped questions.

Q.	Ans.	Correct	Skipped
1	A	43.2 %	1.26 %
2	A	49.7 %	1.15 %
3	A	53.38 %	1.68 %
4	B	42.05 %	1.23 %
5	B	44.15 %	1.59 %
6	C	59.77 %	1.57 %
7	C	49.88 %	1.79 %
8	A	63.39 %	1.09 %
9	B	48.01 %	1.95 %
10	B	68.61 %	1.83 %
11	A	46.45 %	1.34 %
12	B	47.65 %	1.17 %
13	C	52.48 %	1.31 %
14	A	49.91 %	1.72 %
15	A	50.61 %	1.21 %
16	A	68.54 %	1.95 %
17	D	46.07 %	1.8 %
18	B	48.27 %	1.54 %
19	D	56.92 %	1.06 %
20	C	42.53 %	1.03 %
21	D	69.38 %	1.35 %
22	C	55.16 %	1.76 %
23	A	67.45 %	1.99 %
24	A	54.25 %	1.86 %
25	A	58.82 %	1.79 %
26	C	45.19 %	1.31 %
27	C	68.8 %	1.44 %
28	D	61.28 %	1.39 %
29	A	52.82 %	1.12 %
30	B	46.81 %	1.37 %
31	A	23.72 %	3.92 %
32	A	22.79 %	3.77 %
33	A	46.83 %	1.08 %
34	A	65.84 %	1.14 %
35	B	88.03 %	0.0 %
36	C	85.86 %	0.0 %
37	A	83.8 %	0.0 %
38	B	57.8 %	1.83 %
39	D	64.23 %	1.28 %
40	B	67.43 %	1.87 %

Performance Analysis	
Avg. Score (%)	60.0%
Toppers Score (%)	72.5%
Your Score	

//Hints and Solutions//

1. In C when you divide the integer with a float without the type casting it gives "Floating Point Exception" error.

A floating point exception is an error that occurs when you try to do something impossible with a floating point number, such as divide by zero.

Similarly, in this pseudocode we are dividing the floating point-number close to zero.

Hence, the correct option is (A).

2. sizeof(x) that is float is 4.

sizeof(y) that is long int is 8.

sizeof(x+y) that also comes out to be float will have size = 4.

Here it is asking sizeof(x) == sizeof(x+y).

i.e 4 == 4

"==" operator gives result 1.

Hence, the correct option is (A).

3. Iteration 1 : rem = 3(987 % 4), num = 98

Iteration 2 : rem = 2(98 % 4), num = 9

Iteration 3 : rem = 1(9 % 4), num = 0

Hence, the correct option is (A).

4. If float variable is declared as an integer type.

Then, it will always give garbage value.

In this pseudocode, the float variable is initialized in a wrong way or in a integer variable type. That's why the code returns the garbage value.

Hence, the correct option is (B).

5. We use args. length when we want to know the length of the array args .length i.e. when we want to know how many arguments were passed to our main method. For example, if the program is supposed to be called with exactly 2 arguments, but args. length is not 2, we can print an error message and exit.

Value of args. length is 0.

So, the loop will not run either of the time.

Therefore, null will be printed.

Hence, the correct option is (B).

6. a = 0x6db7

b = 0xa726

Both a and b values are hexadecimal value.

= 0110 1101 1011 0111 ^ 1010 0111 0010 0110

= 1100 1010 1001 0001

= 0xca91

= 51857 (in decimal).

Hence, the correct option is (C).

7. x = 4 % -5 + 6 % 5

⇒ x = 4 + 6 % 5

⇒ x = 4 + 1

⇒ x = 5

It is an expression stored in a variable x in the given pseudocode. The operations performed in the given expression are Modulus, Addition, and Subtraction. So, after the execution, the output is 5.

Hence, the correct option is (C).

8. There are two types of variables:

- Global variable
- Local variable

Local variable is declared inside a function whereas Global variable is declared outside the function. Local variables are created when the function has started execution and is lost when the function terminates, on the other hand, Global variable is created as execution starts and is lost when the program ends.

Hence, the correct option is (A).

9. In C++, you can create a constant reference that refers to a constant. To understand it in more, you can consider the following program given as an example.

```
#include<iostream>

using namespace std;
int main()
{
const int x = 10;
const int & ref = x;
cout<< ref;
return 0;
}
```

Hence, the correct option is (B).

10. Whenever a function returns by the reference, it can also be used as the lvalue. However, x is declared as the static variable, it is shared among function calls, but the initialization line "static variable x= 10;" is executed only once. Therefore, the function call " fun()=30, changed the x to 30, and next call "cout<<fun( )" simply returns the updated or modified value. So, the correct answer will be the 30.

Hence, the correct option is (B).

11. In general, a copy constructor is called when the object is passed by the value. You may know that, the copy constructor itself also a type of function. So, if we pass an argument by value in a copy constructor, a call to copy constructor would be made to call copy constructor, which becomes a non-terminating chain of calls. Therefore, compiler doesn't allow parameters to be passed by value.

Hence, the correct option is (A).

12. In Java, an exception caused by other exceptions is known as a chained exception. Generally, the first exception causes the second exception. It helps in identifying the cause of the exception. In chained exceptions, the debugging information is not discarded.

Hence, the correct option is (B).

13. When a String is created using a new operator, it always created in the heap memory. Whereas when we create a string using double quotes, it will check for the same value as of the string in the string constant pool. If it is found, returns a reference of it else create a new string in the string constant pool.

Hence, the correct option is (C).

14. If only single argument is passed to the range method, Python considers this argument as the end of the range and the default start value of range is 0. So, it will print all the numbers starting from 0 and before the supplied argument.

For the second for loop the starting value is explicitly supplied as 4 and ending is 5.

So, the output is-

0
1
4
5

Hence, the correct option is (A).

15. The function "filter" will return all items from list values which return True when passed to the function "checknums". "checknums" will check if the value is in the set. Since all the numbers in the set come from the values list, all of the original values in the list will return True.

Hence, the correct option is (A)

16. Member functions are the functions, which have their declaration inside the class definition and works on the data members of the class. The definition of member functions can be inside or outside the definition of class.

If the member function is defined inside the class definition it can be defined directly, but if its defined outside the class, then we have to use the scope resolution :: operator along with class name along with function name.

For example:

```
class Cube
{
public:
int side;
/*
Declaring function getVolume
with no argument and return type int.
*/
int getVolume();
};
```

Hence, the correct option is (A).

17. An array is a collection of items stored at contiguous memory locations. The idea is to store multiple items of the same type together. This makes it easier to calculate the position of each element by simply adding an offset to a base value, i.e., the memory location of the first element of the array (generally denoted by the name of the array). The base value is index 0 and the difference between the two indexes is the offset.

Syntax: fee[0].amount=feel[0].amount+2;

Hence, the correct option is (D).

18. A virtual function is a member function that is declared within a base class and redefined by a derived class. When a class containing a virtual function is inherited, the derived class redefines the virtual function to suit its own needs. Only those functions are used to achieve the polymorphism, which are declared as 'virtual'. These functions let the OOPS programs decide at runtime which function is to be called by the pointer.

Hence, the correct option is (B).

19. All-access the same function definition as present in the code segment. The compiler supplies an implicit pointer along with the names of the functions as 'this'. The 'this' pointer is passed as a hidden argument to all nonstatic member function calls and is available as a local variable within the body of all nonstatic functions. 'this' pointer is not available in static member functions as static member functions can be called without any object (with class name).

Hence, the correct option is (D).

20. In computer science, a float is a data type composed of a number that is not an integer, because it includes a fraction represented in decimal format. They are technically stored as two integer values: a mantissa and an exponent.

Hence, the correct option is (C).

21. Physical network topology examples include star, mesh, tree, ring, point-to-point, circular, hybrid, and bus topology networks, each consisting of different configurations of nodes and links. The ideal network topology depends on each business's size, scale, goals, and budget. A peer to Peer network is a network to which all computers are used the same resources and rights as other computers. Its network designed primarily for the small local area.

Hence, the correct option is (D).

22. IPv4 addresses are 32-bit numbers that are typically displayed in dotted decimal notation. A 32-bit address contains two primary parts: the network prefix and the host number. All hosts within a single network share the same network address. Each host also has an address that uniquely identifies it.

$\therefore$ Total length = Length of header + Data (16 bits), which has a minimum value of 20 bytes, and the maximum is $2^{16} = 65536$ bytes.

Hence, the correct option is (C).

23. The term IANA stands for Internet Assigned Numbers Authority. IANA, the Internet Assigned Numbers Authority, is an administrative function of the Internet that keeps track of IP addresses, domain names, and protocol parameter identifiers that are used by Internet standards. IANA manages Internet protocol numbering systems in conjunction with relevant standards bodies. At its core, the Internet works by passing data between different computers using a system of unique computer identifiers called IP addresses.

Hence, the correct option is (A).

24. The DNIC has three digits to identify the country (one to identify a zone and two to identify the country within the zone) and one to identify the PDN (allowing only ten in each country). The first three digits of the Data Network Identification Code (DNIC) identify the country (first digit to identify a zone and other two digits to identify the country within the zone).

Hence, the correct option is (A).

25. Modem is short for "Modulator/Demodulator" that allows a computer or other device, such as a router or switch, to connect to the Internet. It converts or "modulates" an analog signal from a telephone or cable wire to a digital signal that a computer can recognize. Similarly, it converts outgoing digital data from a computer or other device to an analog signal.

Hence, the correct option is (A).

26. It is not always possible to decompose a table in BCNF and preserve dependencies. For example, a set of functional dependencies {AB –> C, C –> B} cannot be decomposed in BCNF.

- Normal forms are used to eliminate or reduce redundancy in database tables.
- BCNF is free from redundancy.
- If all attributes of relation are prime attributes, then the relation is always in 3NF.
- A relation in a Relational Database is always and at least in 1NF form.

Hence, the correct option is (C).

27. The DELETE command is used to delete specified rows(one or more). While this command is used to delete all the rows from a table. In data manipulation language, the command like select, insert, update, and delete is used to manipulate the information (or data, records), for example, create a table, update table delete table, etc.

Hence, the correct option is (C).

28. ER model stands for an Entity-Relationship model. It is a high-level data model. This model is used to define the data elements and relationships for a specified system. It develops a conceptual design for the database. It also develops a very simple and easy-to-design view of data. For eg., Suppose an instructor entity set had attributes dept name and dept address, and there is a functional dependency dept name -> dept address.

Hence, the correct option is (D).

29. From the given set of functional dependencies, it can be observed that B is a candidate key of R. So all 200 values of B must be unique in R. There is no functional dependency given for S. To get the maximum number of tuples in output, there can be two possibilities for S.

1) All 100 values of B in S are the same and there is an entry in R that matches with this value. In this case, we get 100 tuples in output.

2) All 100 values of B in S are different and these values are present in R also. In this case, also, we get 100 tuples.

Hence, the correct option is (A).

30. The "COUNT" keyword is used to find the total number of values inside a column. So, whenever a user wants to find the total values in a column, he can use the keyword "COUNT". The keyword density is the percentage of times a keyword appears in a text compared to the total number of words in that text. Simply write or paste your text here and hit "COUNT".

Hence, the correct option is (B).

31. DELETE is used to remove existing records from the database. DELETE command is a DML statement so that it can be rolled back.

DROP is used to DELETE the whole table, including its structure. DROP is a DDL command that lost the data permanently, and it cannot be rolled back.

TRUNCATE is used to DELETE the whole records, but it preserves the table's schema or structure. TRUNCATE is a DDL command, So, it cannot be rolled back.

Hence, the correct option is (A).

32. Candidate key in SQL is a set of fields that identify each record in a table uniquely. It is a super key with no repeated fields that means the minimal super key is a candidate key. A table can contain multiple candidate keys, but it can have only a single primary key.

Hence, the correct option is (A).

33. In MS-DOS, relocatable object files and load modules have extensions is .OBJ and .COM or .EXE, respectively.

.OBJ: OBJ is a geometry definition file format first developed by Wavefront Technologies for its Advanced Visualizer animation package.

.COM: The domain name com is a top-level domain in the Domain Name System of the Internet. Its name is derived from the word commercial, indicating its original intended purpose for domains registered by commercial organizations.

.EXE: EXE is a file extension for an executable file format. An executable is a file that contains a program - that is, a particular kind of file that is capable of being executed or run as a program in the computer. An executable file can be run by a program in Microsoft DOS or Windows through a command or a double click.

Hence, the correct option is (A).

34. The state transition initiated by the user process itself in an operating system is block. A block is a contiguous set of bits or bytes that forms an identifiable unit of data. The term is used in database management, word processing, and network communication. It is a multiple of an operating system block, which is the smallest amount of data that can be retrieved from storage or memory.

Hence, the correct option is (A).

35. Wrap is the attribute of <textarea> element and it indicates whether the text should be wrapped.

Syntax: <textarea wrap="">

if we use wrap="hard" it will contain newlines in the submission of a form. This attribute is newly introduced by HTML5 and is supported by all the browsers.

Hence, the correct option is (B).

36. <button>, <li>, <progress>, <param>, <meter>, <input>, <option> are some elements used with value attribute and defines a default value on the page load. <object> element is used with many attributes like border, data, form, height etc. <area> is used with attributes like alt, cords, download, href, hreflang and many more.

Hence, the correct option is (C).

37. The title is a global attribute that displays text in a tooltip when hovered over the element.

Syntax is: <element title="text">

The title attribute can be used on any HTML element (it will validate on any HTML element. However, it is not necessarily useful). The title global attribute contains text representing advisory information related to the element it belongs to.

Hence, the correct option is (A).

38. The feedback paths allow the phase to be reworked in which errors are committed and these changes are reflected in the later phases. But, there is no feedback path to the stage–feasibility study, because once a project has been taken, does not give up the project easily.

It is good to detect errors in the same phase in which they are committed. It reduces the effort and time required to correct the errors.

Hence, the correct option is (B).

39. The Prototyping model is also a popular software development life cycle model. This model suggests building a working prototype of the system, before the development of the actual software. A prototype is a toy and crude implementation of a system. The Prototyping Model should be used when the requirements of the product are not clearly understood or are unstable. It can also be used if requirements are changing quickly.

Hence, the correct option is (D).

40. The wildcard is a character used to search complex data from the database quickly. We can use it in conjunction with the LIKE or NOT LIKE comparison operators and the WHERE clause to find the result for a specified pattern. So, the wildcard is very useful when the exact match is not possible in the SELECT statement.

Hence, the correct option is (B).

Mock Test 07

Q.1 Consider the following C function:

```
int tmp;
tmp = x;
x = y;
y = tmp;
```

In order to exchange the values of two variables a and b:

A. Call swap (a, b)
B. Call swap (&a, &b)
C. Swap(a, b) cannot be used as it does not return any value.
D. Swap(a, b) cannot be used as the parameters passed by value.

Q.2 What is correct about the below program?

```
int i;
int main()
{
if (i);
else
printf("Ëlse");
return 0;
}
```

A. If block is executed.
B. Else block is executed.
C. It is unpredictable as i is not initialized.
D. Error: misplaced else.

Q.3 What is output of following code?

```
Integer x,y
Set x=25 , y=5
print(x)
LABEL : x = x + ++y
if(x<50)
print(x)
goto label
END if
print(y)
```

A. 25 31 36 46 54 **B.** 25 31 38 46 9
C. 25 30 35 45 9 **D.** None of these

Q.4 What is output of following code. if m=8,n=2:

```
n = -n
m=++m
if(m >= n)
if(m == 0)
print(m+n)
END if
else if(m >= n)
if(m != 0)
print(m-n)
```

A. 8 **B.** 10
C. 6 **D.** No Output

Q.5 What will be the output of the following Python code?

```
>>>a={"a":1,"b":2,"c":3}
>>>b=dict(zip(a.values(),a.keys()))
>>>b
```

A. {'a': 1, 'b': 2, 'c': 3}
B. An exception is thrown
C. {'a': 'b': 'c': }
D. {1: 'a', 2: 'b', 3: 'c'}

Q.6 Study the following program:

```
main()
{
printf("national");
main();
}
```

What will be the output of this program?

A. Wrong statement
B. It will keep on printing national
C. It will Print national once
D. None of the these

Q.7 Which of the following functions allocates multiple blocks of memory, each block of the same size?

A. malloc() **B.** realloc() **C.** calloc() **D.** free()

Q.8 Which of the following best describes the ordering of destructor calls for stack-resident objects in a routine?

A. The first object created is the first object destroyed; last created is last destroyed.
B. The first object destroyed is the last object destroyed; last created is first destroyed.
C. Objects are destroyed in the order they appear in memory, the object with the lowest memory address is destroyed first.
D. The order is undefined and may vary from compiler to compiler.

Q.9 How many bytes does "int = D" use?

A. 0 **B.** 1 **C.** 2 or 4 **D.** 10

Q.10 What will the result of len variable after execution of the following statements?

```
int len;
char str1[] = {"39 march road"};
len = strlen(str1);
```

A. 11 **B.** 12 **C.** 13 **D.** 14

Q.11 Return a value:

```
print("Welcome to EduGorilla.")
a = 10
# Two objects are passed in print() function
print("a =", a)
b = a
# Three objects are passed in print function
print('a =', a, '= b')
```

A. Welcome to EduGorilla.

a = 10
a = 10 = b
b = a = 10

B. 10 = b
Welcome to Edu
10 = a = b

C. 10 = b
Welcome to EduG

D. None of the above

Q.12 Using sep and end argument return a value:

```
a = 10
print("a =", a, sep='dddd', end='\n\n\n')
print("a =", a, sep='0', end='$$$$$')
```

A. a =010$$$$$
a =dddd10

B. a =$$$$$010
a =10dddd

C. a =dddd10
a =010$$$$$

D. Error

Q.13 What will be the output of the following Python code?

```
count={}
count[(1,2,4)] = 5
count[(4,2,1)] = 7
count[(1,2)] = 6
count[(4,2,1)] = 2
tot = 0
for i in count:
  tot=tot+count[i]
print(len(count)+tot)
```

A. 25
B. 17
C. 16
D. Tuples can't be made keys of a dictionary

Q.14 A condition where in memory is reserved dynamically but not accessible to any of the programs is called ___________.

A. Memory leak **B.** Dangling pointer
C. Frozen memory **D.** Pointer leak

Q.15 From which tag descriptive list starts?

A. <LL> **B.** <DD> **C.** <DL> **D.** <DS>

Q.16 Can the element<First>be replaced with<first>.

A. No, they represent different elements altogether
B. Both are same
C. First is correct only
D. first is only correct

Q.17 Any part of the graphic that is not included in another hot zone is considered to be part of-

A. Rect **B.** Point **C.** Default **D.** Polygon

Q.18 The data blocks of a very large file in the Unix file system are allocated using:

A. Contiguous allocation
B. Linked allocation
C. Indexed allocation
D. An extension of indexed allocation

Q.19 Direction: In the following process state transition diagram for a uniprocessor system, assume that there are always some processes in the ready state: Now consider the following statements:

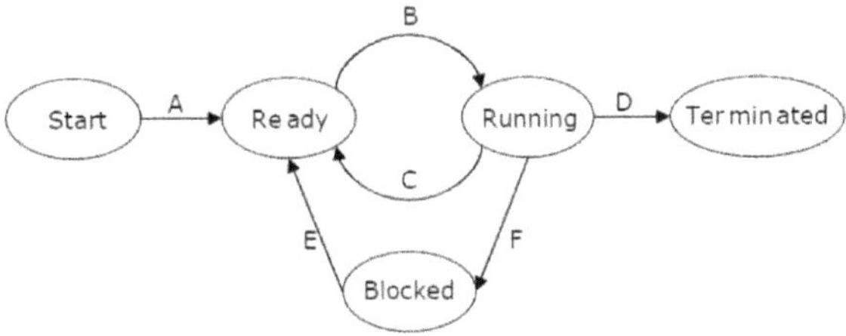

I. If a process makes a transition D, it would result in another process making transition A immediately.

II. A process P2 in blocked state can make transition E while another process P1 is in running state.

III. The OS uses preemptive scheduling.

IV. The OS uses non-preemptive scheduling.

Which of the above statements are TRUE?

A. I and II **B.** I and III **C.** II and III **D.** II and IV

Q.20 If an attribute of a composite key is dependent on an attribute of the other composite key, a normalization called ____ is needed.

A. DKNF **B.** BCNF **C.** Fourth **D.** Third

Q.21 Which one of the following is NOT desired in a good Software Requirement Specifications (SRS) document?

A. Functional Requirements
B. Non-Functional Requirements
C. Goals of Implementation
D. Algorithms for Software Implementation

Q.22 Which among the following is best to define hierarchical inheritance?

A. More than one classes being derived from one class.
B. More than 2 classes being derived from single base class.
C. At most 2 classes being derived from single base class.
D. At most 1 class derived from another class.

Q.23 Which access specifiers should be used so that all the derived classes restrict further inheritance of base class members?

A. Private
B. Public
C. Protected
D. Any inheritance type can be used

Q.24 Which of the following statement is true?

I) In Procedural programming languages, all function calls are resolved at compile-time.

II) In Object Oriented programming languages, all function calls are resolved at compile-time.

A. I only **B.** II only
C. Both I and II **D.** Neither I nor II

Q.25 How many types of polymorphism in the C++ programming language?

A. Three types of polymorphism

B. Two types of polymorphism
C. Five types of polymorphism
D. Four types of polymorphism

Q.26 Which operator overloads using the friend function?

A. * **B.** () **C.** -> **D.** =

Q.27 A ______ is a property of the entire relation rather than of the individual tuples in which each tuple is unique.

A. Key **B.** Rows **C.** Attribute **D.** Fields

Q.28 You are connecting your access point and it is set to root. What does Extended Service Set ID mean?

A. That you have more than one access point and they are in the same SSID connected by a distribution system.
B. That you have more than one access point and they are in separate SSIDs connected by a distribution system.
C. That you have multiple access points, but they are placed physically in different buildings.
D. That you have multiple access points, but one is a repeater access point.

Q.29 The smallest logical data entity is called a data item or data-

A. Field **B.** Collection
C. Base **D.** Bank

Q.30 What is a Module?

A. a collection of declarations, statements, and procedures
B. it is a machine language
C. it is a low-level language
D. None of the above

Q.31 Which of these is considered intelligent CASE tool?

A. Upper CASE
B. Methodology companion
C. Workbench
D. Lower CASE

Q.32 A station in a network forwards incoming packets by placing them on its shortest output queue. What routing algorithm is being used?

A. Hot potato routing **B.** Flooding
C. Static routing **D.** Delta routing

Q.33 Frames from one LAN can be transmitted to another LAN via the device:

A. Router **B.** Bridge **C.** Repeater **D.** Modem

Q.34 What is the port number for NNTP?

A. 119 **B.** 80 **C.** 79 **D.** 70

Q.35 Usually, it takes 10-bits to represent one character. How many characters can be transmitted at a speed of 1200 BPS?

A. 10 **B.** 12 **C.** 120 **D.** 1200

Q.36 The ____ houses the switches in token ring.

A. Transceiver **B.** Nine-pin connector
C. MAU **D.** NIC

Q.37 Which of the following is an explicit numeric, character, string, or BOOLEAN value not represented by an identifier?

A. Delimiters **B.** Literals
C. Comments **D.** None of the above

Q.38 How to select all data from student table starting the name from letter 'r'?

A. SELECT * FROM student WHERE name LIKE 'r%';
B. SELECT * FROM student WHERE name LIKE '%r%';
C. SELECT * FROM student WHERE name LIKE '%r';
D. SELECT * FROM student WHERE name LIKE '_r%';

Q.39 What operator tests column for the absence of data?

A. EXISTS operator **B.** NOT operator
C. IS NULL operator **D.** None of these

Q.40 The free() function frees the memory state pointed to by a pointer and returns _________.

A. The same pointer
B. The memory address
C. No value
D. An integer value

// Smart Answer Sheet //

Correct — Indicates percentage of students who answered questions correctly.

Skipped — Indicates percentage of students who skipped questions.

Q.	Ans.	Correct	Skipped
1	D	63.12 %	1.85 %
2	B	13.89 %	4.71 %
3	B	61.48 %	1.8 %
4	D	79.02 %	0.0 %
5	D	13.97 %	4.58 %
6	B	44.73 %	1.6 %
7	C	50.58 %	1.08 %
8	B	60.21 %	1.66 %
9	C	89.06 %	0.0 %
10	C	80.17 %	0.0 %
11	A	18.41 %	4.97 %
12	C	31.74 %	3.69 %
13	C	14.66 %	4.22 %
14	A	44.52 %	1.67 %
15	C	89.67 %	0.0 %
16	B	56.15 %	1.33 %
17	C	68.91 %	1.39 %
18	D	18.75 %	4.61 %
19	C	29.06 %	4.13 %
20	B	63.57 %	1.78 %
21	D	50.62 %	1.53 %
22	A	77.6 %	0.0 %
23	A	84.96 %	0.0 %
24	A	52.42 %	1.56 %
25	B	78.32 %	0.0 %
26	A	41.74 %	1.91 %
27	A	41.18 %	1.14 %
28	A	89.23 %	0.0 %
29	A	43.52 %	1.69 %
30	A	40.27 %	1.05 %
31	C	59.18 %	1.3 %
32	A	25.04 %	4.12 %
33	B	51.49 %	1.86 %
34	A	27.83 %	4.27 %
35	C	27.8 %	4.73 %
36	C	57.54 %	1.78 %
37	B	77.14 %	0.0 %
38	A	59.68 %	1.11 %
39	C	77.69 %	0.0 %
40	C	41.66 %	1.76 %

Performance Analysis	
Avg. Score (%)	45.0%
Toppers Score (%)	55.0%
Your Score	

//Hints and Solutions//

1. The code will not work because the parameters are passed by value. In order to swap the values of x and y, the parameters should be passed with reference. The correct code is:

```
void swap ( int &x, int &y )
{
int tmp;
tmp = x;
x = y;
y = tmp;
}
```

Hence, the correct option is (D).

2. Since i is defined globally, it is initialized with default value 0. The else block is executed as the expression within if evaluates to FALSE. An empty block is equivalent to a semi-colon(;).

So, the statements if (i);and if (i) {} are equivalent.

Hence, the correct option is (B).

3. In this above code, we use the number of steps these are:-

Step 1:- The value of x=25.

Step 2:- Now , the value of x becomes 31 ;due to the expression : x=x+ ++y =25+6=31 (∵++y=5+1=6).

And IF condition i.e. x should be less than 50.

Step 3:- Now, the value of x becomes 38; for the given above same reason.

Step 4:- Now, the value of x becomes 46; for the given above same reason.

Step 5:- Finally, in this step, there does not the value of x but the value y exists i.e. y=9 due to the IF condition given in above code and the execution of the code.

So, the output is 25 31 38 46 9.

Hence, the correct option is (B).

4. In the following code, the output is No Output because of the given first statement in the following code i.e. n=-n; which is an invalid statement and the condition becomes false in the first line of the code. Therefore, the loop terminates by default.

For this the correct code should be :-

```
n-=n
m=++m
if(m>=n)
if(m==0)
print(m+n)
END if
else if (m>=n)
if(m!=0)
print(m-n)
```

Hence, the correct option is (D).

5. The above piece of code inverts the key-value pairs in the dictionary. Dictionary in Python is an unordered collection of datavalues, used to store data values like a map, which unlike other Data Typesthat hold only single value as an element, Dictionary holds key:value pair. This method will create a new key:value pair on a dictionary by assigning avalue to that key.

Use items() to Reverse a Dictionary in Python.

Reverse the key-value pairs bylooping the result of items() and switching the key and the value.

Hence, the correct option is (D).

6. In this program, the main function will call itself again and again. Therefore, it will continue to print national. You can use the "return" command to return values to the function call. Python will print a random value like (0x021B2D30) when the argument is not supplied to the calling function.

Hence, the correct option is (B).

7. calloc() allocates multiple blocks of memory, each block with the same size. The calloc() function in C is used to allocate a specified amount of memory and then initialize it to zero. The function returns a void pointer to this memory location, which can then be cast to the desired type. The function takes in two parameters that collectively specify the amount of memory to be allocated.

Hence, the correct option is (C).

8. The first object destroyed is the last object destroyed; last created is first destroyed are describes the ordering of destructor calls for stack-resident objects in a routine. A destructor is called for a class object when that object passes out of scope or is explicitly deleted. A destructor can be declared virtual or pure virtual.

Hence, the correct option is (B).

9. The int type takes 2 or 4 bytes. D provides a 32-bit and 64-bit data model for use in writing programs. The size of an int is really compiler dependent. Back in the day, when processors were 16 bit, an int was 2 bytes. Nowadays, it's most often 4 bytes on a 32-bit as well as 64-bit systems. Still, using sizeof(int) is the best way to get the size of an integer for the specific system the program is executed on.

Hence, the correct option is (C).

10. Strlen is a string function that counts the word and also count the space in the string. (39 march road) = 13.

The strlen() is a built-in function in PHP which returns the length of a given string. It takes a string as a parameter and returns its length. It calculates the length of the string including all the whitespaces and special characters.

Hence, the correct option is (C).

11. Return is a reserved keyword in Java i.e, we can't use it as an identifier. It is used to exit from a method, with or without a value.

Output:

```
Welcome to EduGorilla.
a = 10
a = 10 = b
```

As we can see in the above output, the multiple objects can be printed in the single print() statement. We just need to use comma (,) to separate with each other.

Hence, the correct option is (A).

12. Output:

a =dddd10
a =010$$$$$

In the first print() statement, we use the sep and end arguments. The given object is printed just after the sep values. The value of end parameter printed at the last of given object. As we can see that, the second print() function printed the result after the three black lines.

Hence, the correct option is (C).

13. Tuples can be made keys of a dictionary. Length of the dictionary is 3 as the value of the key (4,2,1) is modified to 2. The value of the variable tot is 5+6+2+3=16.

Tuple objects are sequences. A dictionary is a hash table of key-value pairs. List and tuple is an ordered collection of items. List and dictionary objects are mutable i.e. it is possible to add new item or delete and item from it. Tuple is an immutable object.

Hence, the correct option is (C).

14. A condition where in memory is reserved dynamically but not accessible to any of the programs is called Memory leak. If we allocate memory dynamically in a function (malloc, calloc, realloc), the allocated memory will not be de-allocated automatically when the control comes out of the function. This allocated memory cannot be accessed. therefore, cannot be used. This unused inaccessible memory results in a memory leak.

Hence, the correct option is (A).

15. HTML tags are like keywords which defines that how web browser will format and display the content. With the help of tags, a web browser can distinguish between an HTML content and a simple content. HTML tags contain three main parts: opening tag, content and closing tag. But some HTML tags are unclosed tags.<DL> tag is sued to define a description list.

For example:

<p>Cryptids of Cornwall:</p>
<dl> <dt>Beast of Bodmin</dt> <dd>A large feline inhabiting Bodmin Moor.</dd> <dt>Morgawr</dt> <dd>A sea serpent.</dd> <dt>Owlman</dt> <dd>A giant owl-like creature.</dd></dl>

Output:

Cryptids of Cornwall:
Beast of Bodmin
A large feline inhabiting Bodmin Moor.
Morgawr
A sea serpent.
Owlman
A giant owl-like creature.

Hence, the correct option is (C).

16. Tag names for HTML elements may be written with any mix of lowercase and uppercase letters that are a case-insensitive match for the names of the elements given in the HTML elements section of this document. that is, tag names are case-insensitive.

The first tag in any HTML file is the <HTML> tag. This tells web browsers that the document is an HTML file. The second tag is a <HEAD> tag. Information between the HEAD tags doesn't appear in the browser window, but is still important.

Hence, the correct option is (B).

17. The default attribute is a boolean attribute. When present, it specifies that the track is to be enabled if the user's preferences do not indicate that another track would be more appropriate.

There must not be more than one <track> element with a default attribute per<media> element.

Hence, the correct option is (C).

18. The Unix file system uses an extension of indexed allocation. It uses direct blocks, single indirect blocks, double indirect blocks and triple indirect blocks.

Following diagram shows implementation of Unix file system:

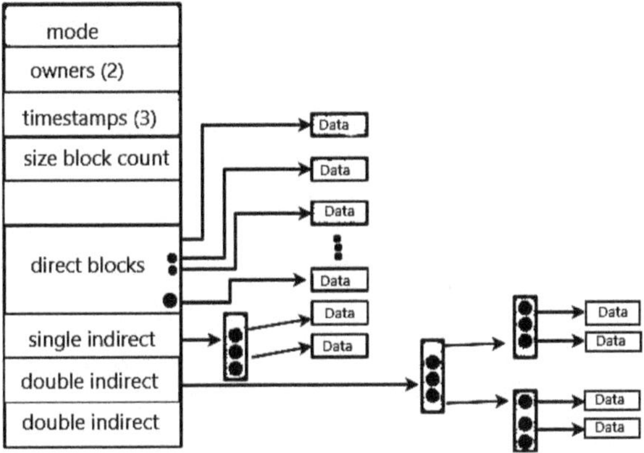

The Unix file system (UFS) is a file system supported by many Unix and Unix-like operating systems. It is a distant descendant of the original filesystem used by Version 7 Unix.

Hence, the correct option is (D).

19. II is true. A process can move to ready state when I/O completes irrespective of other process being in running state or not.

III is true because there is a transition from running to ready state.

IV is false as the OS uses preemptive scheduling.

I is false. If a process makes a transition D, it would result in another process making transition B, not A.

Hence, the correct option is (C).

20. BCNF eliminates all redundancy that can be discovered based on functional dependencies. BCNF is the advance version of 3NF. It is stricter than 3NF. A table is in BCNF if every functional dependency X → Y, X is the super key of the table. For BCNF, the table should be in 3NF, and for every FD, LHS is super key.

Hence, the correct option is (B).

21. Algorithms for Software Implementation is not desired in a good Software Requirement Specifications (SRS) document. A software requirements specification (SRS) is a description of a software system to be developed. The software requirements specification lays out functional and non-functional requirements, and it may include a set of use cases that describe user interactions that the software must provide.

Hence, the correct option is (D).

22. When two or more classes get derived from a single base class, it is known as hierarchical inheritance. This gives us freedom to use same code with different scopes and flexibility into different classes.

Hierarchical inheritance is a kind of inheritance where more than one class is inherited from a single parent or base class. Especially those features which are common in the parent class is also common with the base class.

Hence, the correct option is (A).

23. All the derived classes must use private inheritance. This will make the members of base class private in derived classes. Hence none of the members of base class will be available for further inheritance.

Private Inheritance is one of the ways of implementing the relationship. With private inheritance, public and protected member of the base class become private members of the derived class. That means the methods of the base class do not become the public interface of the derived object.

Hence, the correct option is (A).

24. In Procedural programming like C we don't have the concept of polymorphism, therefore, all the function calls are resolved at the compile-time but in case of OOP languages sue to polymorphism concept all function calls are not resolved at compile-time.

Hence, the correct option is (A).

25. C++ programming language has two types of polymorphism: 1. Runtime Polymorphism 2. Compile-time Polymorphism.

Runtime Polymorphism: It is meet by the function overriding. This polymorphism is also known as late or dynamic binding.

Compile-time Polymorphism: It is meet by the operator and function overloading. This polymorphism is also known as early or static binding.

Hence, the correct option is (B).

26. The operators (->, (), =) cannot be overloaded using the friend function because if they are overloaded, then the code will show the compilation error. That's why * (asterisk) is a symbol that can be overloaded using the friend function.

In object-oriented programming, a friend function, that is a "friend" of a given class, is a function that is given the same access as methods to private and protected data. A friend function is declared by the class that is granting access, so friend functions are part of the class interface, like methods.

Hence, the correct option is (A).

27. A key is a property of the entire relation rather than of the individual tuples in which each tuple is unique.

A key in DBMS is an attribute or a set of attributes that help to uniquely identify a tuple (or row) in a relation (or table). Keys are also used to establish relationships between the different tables and columns of a relational database. Individual values in a key are called key values.

Hence, the correct option is (A).

28. Extended Service Set ID means that you have more than one access point and they all are set to the same SSID and all are connected together in the same VLAN or distribution system so users can roam. An Extended Service Set is comprised of a number of IEEE 802.11 BSS (Basic Service Set) and enables limited mobility within the WiFi network. Stations are able to move between BSS within a single ESS yet still remain connected to the fixed network and so continue to receive emails etc.

Hence, the correct option is (A).

29. The smallest logical data entity is called a data item or data field.

A field consists of a grouping of characters. A data field represents an attribute (a characteristic or quality) of some entity (object, person, place, or event).

Data stored in computer systems form a hierarchy extending from a single bit to a database, the major record-keeping entity of a firm. Bit (Character) - a bit is the smallest unit of data representation (value of a bit may be a 0 or 1).

Hence, the correct option is (A).

30. A module is a collection of declarations, statements, and procedures that are stored together as a unit. Modules are very similar to Macros since they are objects that add functionality to the database.

Class modules are attached to forms or reports, and usually contain procedures that are specific to the form or report they're attached to. Standard modules contain general procedures that aren't associated with any other object. Standard modules are listed under Modules in the Navigation Pane, whereas class modules are not.

Hence, the correct option is (A).

31. Workbench is considered intelligent CASE tool. Various tools are incorporated in CASE and are called CASE tools, which are used to support different stages and milestones in a software development life cycle.

Hence, the correct option is (C).

32. In Isolated method, each node makes its routing decisions using the information it has without seeking information from other nodes. The sending nodes doesn't have information about status of particular link. Disadvantage is that packet may be sent through a congested network which may result in delay.

Examples: Hot potato routing, backward learning.

Hence, the correct option is (A).

33. A bridge is a network device that connects multiple LANs (local area networks) together to form a larger LAN. A bridge connects the different components so that they appear as parts of a single network. Bridges operate at the data link layer of the OSI model and hence also referred as Layer 2 switches.

Bridges are used to connect two or more hosts or network segments together. The basic role of bridges in network architecture is storing and forwarding frames between the different segments that the bridge connects. They use hardware Media Access Control (MAC) addresses for transferring frames.

Hence, the correct option is (B).

34. The port number for NNTP is 119. The Network News Transfer Protocol (NNTP) is an application protocol used for transporting Usenet news articles (netnews) between news servers, and for reading/posting articles by the end user client applications.

Hence, the correct option is (A).

35. Such questions are case sensitive, B = Bytes, b = bits, and 1 Byte = 8 bit.

One character =10 bit.

1200 bit = 120 character.

Therefore, in 1 sec 120 character transfer.

BPS means 8 bits PS as 1 byte = 8 bits or you mean byte = 10 bit for this case.

Hence, the correct option is (C).

36. The MAU houses the switches in token ring. A media access unit (MAU), also known as a multistation access unit (MAU or MSAU), is a device to attach multiple network stations in a star topology as a Token Ring network, internally wired to connect the stations into a logical ring (generally passive i.e. non-switched and unmanaged; however managed Token Ring MAU.

Hence, the correct option is (C).

37. Literals are similar to the constants. There are 4 types of literals-

1. Text literals
2. Integer literals
3. Number
4. Date/Time literals.

Hence, the correct option is (B).

38. By using LIKE query we can match part of the full data present in a column. Here our search word need not exactly match.

Using Like Query with wildcard in different combinations, we can match our keyword with the pattern of the data present in columns.

The best way to use LIKE command is to apply it against a text or varchar field along with wildcard (%or_).

Hence, the correct option is (A).

39. Always use IS NULL to look for NULL values.

Syntax:
SELECT "column_name"
FROM "table_name"
WHERE "column_name" IS NULL

Hence, the correct option is (C).

40. The free() function frees the memory state pointed by a pointer and returns no value.

The term free function in C++ simply refers to non-member functions. Every function that is not a member function is a free function.

The free() function in C library allows you to release or deallocate the memory blocks which are previously allocated by calloc(), malloc() or realloc() functions. It frees up the memory blocks and returns the memory to heap. It helps freeing the memory in your program which will be available for later use.

Hence, the correct option is (C).

Mock Test 08

Q.1 What will be the output of the following Java code?

```
int arr[] = new int [5];
System.out.print(arr);
```

A. 0
B. Value stored in arr[0]
C. 00000
D. Class name@ hashcode in hexadecimal form

Q.2 What will be the output of the following Java code?

```
class array_output
{
public static void main(String args[])
{
int array_variable [] = new int[20];
for (int i = 0; i< 20; ++i)
{
array_variable[i] = i;
System.out.print(array_variable[i] + " ");
i++;
}
}
}
```

A. 0 2 4 6 8 10 12 14 16 18
B. 1 3 5 7 9
C. 0 2 4 6 8
D. None of these

Q.3 What will be the output of the following Java code?

```
class evaluate
{
public static void main(String args[])
{
int arr[] = new int[] {0 , 1, 2, 3, 4, 5, 6, 7, 8, 9};
int n = 6;
n = arr[arr[n] / 2];
System.out.println(arr[n] / 2);
}
}
```

A. 3 **B.** 0 **C.** 6 **D.** 1

Q.4 Let A and B be objects of class Foo. Which functions are called when print(A + B) is executed?

A. __add__(), __str__()
B. __str__(), __add__()
C. __sum__(), __str__()
D. __str__(), __sum__()

Q.5 Which operator is overloaded by __lg__()?

A. <
B. >
C. !=
D. None of the mentioned

Q.6 Which of the following is correct?

A. Struct tag is required in both C and C++ while declaring an object of the structure.
B. Struct is not required in C but required in C++ while declaring an object of the structure.
C. Struct is not required in C++ but required in C while declaring an object of the structure.
D. Struct tag is not required in both C and C++ while declaring an object of the structure.

Q.7 What happens if the following program is compiled in both C and C++?

```
#include<stdio.h>
struct STRUCT
{
int static a;
};
int main()
{
struct STRUCT s;
return 0;
}
```

A. The program runs fine and both prints output "HELLO THIS IS STRUCTURE".
B. The program gives an error in case of C but runs perfectly in case of C++.
C. The program gives an error in case of C++ but runs perfectly in case of C.
D. The program gives an error in case of both C and C++.

Q.8 Which of the following is a stringizing operator?

A. < > **B.** # **C.** % **D.** ##

Q.9 What will be the output of the following C code?

```
#define display(a) #a
main()
{
printf(display("56#7"));
}
```

A. Error **B.** "56#7" **C.** 56#7 **D.** 567

Q.10 What will be the output of the following C code?

```
#define hello(c) #c
main()
{
printf(hello(i,am));
}
```

A. i,am **B.** iam **C.** i am **D.** Error

Q.11 What is the correct syntax of declaring array of pointers of integers of size 10 in C++?

A. int arr = new int[10];
B. int **arr = new int*[10];
C. int *arr = new int[10];
D. int *arr = new int*[10];

Q.12 Which of the following is correct about new and malloc?

i) New is an operator whereas malloc is a function.

ii) New calls constructor malloc does not.

iii) New returns required pointer whereas malloc returns void pointer and needs to be typecast.

A. i and ii **B.** ii and iii
C. i and iii **D.** i, ii and iii

Q.13 Which of the following explains the overloading of functions?

A. Virtual polymorphism
B. Transient polymorphism
C. Ad-hoc polymorphism
D. Pseudo polymorphism

Q.14 Which of the following is true?

I) All operators in C++ can be overloaded.

II) The basic meaning of an operator can be changed.

A. I only **B.** II only
C. Both I and II **D.** Neither I nor II

Q.15 Which among the following is true?

A. Hierarchical inheritance is subset of multiple inheritances.
B. Hierarchical inheritance is strongest inheritance type.
C. Hierarchical inheritance uses only 2 classes for implementation.
D. Hierarchical inheritance allows inheritance of common features to more than one class.

Q.16 Success callback function evoke only when _________.

A. User accepts to share location information
B. Always evoke
C. Gps is accessible
D. Only by mobile browser

Q.17 Which of the following property does not has always a return?

A. coords.longitude **B.** coords.latitude
C. coords.accuracy **D.** coords.altitude

Q.18 What is the default value of setTimeout?

A. infinity **B.** 100 **C.** 0 **D.** 1000000

Q.19 What is the priority of a real-time task?

A. Must degrade over time.
B. Must not degrade over time.
C. May degrade over time.
D. None of the mentioned

Q.20 The technique in which the CPU generates physical addresses directly is known as _________.

A. Relocation register method
B. Real addressing
C. Virtual addressing
D. None of the mentioned

Q.21 The expected value for the estimation variable (size), S, can be computed as a weighted average of the optimistic(Sopt), most likely (Sm), and pessimistic (Spess) estimates given as:

A. EV = (Sopt + 4Sm + Spess)/4
B. EV = (Sopt + 4Sm + Spess)/6
C. EV = (Sopt + 2Sm + Spess)/6
D. EV = (Sopt + 2Sm + Spess)/4

Q.22 How many forms exists of Barry Boehm's COCOMO Model?

A. Two **B.** Three
C. Four **D.** No form exists

Q.23 Snapshot isolation is a particular type of ___________ scheme.

A. Concurrency-control
B. Concurrency-allowanc
C. Redirection
D. Repetition-allowance

Q.24 Under first updater wins the system uses a ________ mechanism that applies only to updates.

A. Close **B.** Read **C.** Locking **D.** Beat

Q.25 An application developer can guard against certain snapshot anomalies by appending a _____ clause to the SQL select query.

A. For update
B. For read
C. For write
D. None of the mentioned

Q.26 Consider a relation R(A,B,C,D,E) with the following functional dependencies:

ABC ->DE and

D ->AB

The number of superkeys of R is:

A. 2 **B.** 7 **C.** 10 **D.** 12

Q.27 The CREATE TRIGGER statement is used to create the trigger. THE ____ clause specifies the table name on which the trigger is to be attached. The _____ specifies that this is an AFTER INSERT trigger.

A. For insert, on **B.** On, for insert
C. For, insert **D.** None of the above

Q.28 Which of the following is used to avoid cascading of authorizations from the user?

A. Granted by current role.
B. Revoke select on department from Amit, Satoshi restrict.
C. Revoke grant option for select on department from Amit.
D. Revoke select on department from Amit, Satoshi cascade.

Q.29 The granting and revoking of roles by the user may cause some confusions when that user role is revoked. To overcome the above situation-

A. The privilege must be granted only by roles.
B. The privilege is granted by roles and users.
C. The user role cannot be removed once given.
D. By restricting the user access to the roles.

Q.30 Which of the following is not true about Sequential Control statements?

A.	Sequential control statements are crucial to PL/SQL programming.
B.	Occasionally, GOTO statement simplifies logic enough to warrant its use.
C.	NULL statement canimprove readability by making the meaning and action of conditional statements clear.
D.	Sequential control statements are used to handle out of the ordinary requirements for sequential processing.

Q.31 Membership in a VLAN can be based on_____________.

A. Port numbers **B.** MAC address
C. IP address **D.** All of the above

Q.32 Configuration management can be divided into two subsystems: reconfiguration and ________.

A. Documentation **B.** Information
C. Servers **D.** Entity

Q.33 Which of the following networks supports pipelining effect?

A. Circuit-switched network
B. Message-switched networks
C. Packet-switched networks
D. Stream-switched networks

Q.34 MIB is a collection of groups of objects that can be managed by ________.

A. SMTP **B.** UDP **C.** SNMP **D.** TCP/IP

Q.35 SSH-2 does not contain ___________.

A. Transport layer
B. User authentication layer
C. Physical layer
D. Connection layer

Q.36 What will be output of given pseudo code:

```
int j=41, k= 37
j=j+1
k=k-1
j=j/k
k=k/j
print(k,j)
```

A. 42 36 **B.** 36 1 **C.** 1 1 **D.** 1 36

Q.37 Find the output of following pseudo code:

```
int main()
{
int a =0,b=1,c=2;
*( ( a+1==1) ? &b : &a)= a? b : c;
printf("%d, %d, %d \n", a , b, c );
return 0;
}
```

A. 0 1 2 **B.** 0 2 0 **C.** 0 2 2 **D.** Error

Q.38 Predict the output of the given pseudo code if the value of number is 6.

```
number = input()
k = 2
i = 2
while i<=number
k = k * i
i = i +1
end while
write k
```

A. 1700 **B.** 1560 **C.** 1440 **D.** Error

Q.39 Find the output of following pseudo code:

```
int main()
{
int num = 8;
printf ("%d %d", num<< 1, num >>1);
return 0;
}
```

A. 8 0
B. 0 0
C. 16 4
D. Error: Can't Perform operation

Q.40 With the given information provided, find out the address of Arr[17] in a 1-D array Arr[30]:

- lower bound = 1
- starting base address = 1100
- size of each element is 2.

A. 1132 **B.** 1070 **C.** 1128 **D.** 1068

// Smart Answer Sheet //

Correct Indicates percentage of students who answered questions correctly.

Skipped Indicates percentage of students who skipped questions.

Q.	Ans.	Correct	Skipped
1	D	32.89 %	3.15 %
2	A	69.54 %	1.32 %
3	D	54.08 %	1.87 %
4	A	49.86 %	1.36 %
5	D	89.08 %	0.0 %
6	C	88.64 %	0.0 %
7	B	48.86 %	1.74 %
8	B	67.69 %	1.16 %
9	B	12.03 %	3.56 %
10	D	59.57 %	1.01 %
11	B	57.62 %	1.04 %
12	D	67.39 %	1.3 %
13	C	19.71 %	4.42 %
14	D	89.16 %	0.0 %
15	D	44.71 %	1.24 %
16	A	23.33 %	4.33 %
17	D	67.76 %	1.65 %
18	A	88.74 %	0.0 %
19	B	80.84 %	0.0 %
20	B	41.84 %	1.76 %
21	B	28.64 %	4.24 %
22	B	44.37 %	1.6 %
23	A	63.55 %	1.89 %
24	C	55.59 %	1.98 %
25	A	42.02 %	1.16 %
26	C	12.61 %	4.63 %
27	B	50.66 %	1.54 %
28	B	12.01 %	3.31 %
29	A	45.52 %	1.28 %
30	A	81.73 %	0.0 %
31	D	46.34 %	1.69 %
32	A	56.96 %	1.97 %
33	C	82.37 %	0.0 %
34	C	60.76 %	1.02 %
35	C	48.85 %	1.28 %
36	D	57.91 %	1.23 %
37	C	19.22 %	3.94 %
38	C	61.96 %	1.16 %
39	C	82.52 %	0.0 %
40	A	24.15 %	4.09 %

Performance Analysis	
Avg. Score (%)	**37.5%**
Toppers Score (%)	**70.0%**
Your Score	

//Hints and Solutions//

1. If we trying to print any reference variable internally, toString() will be called which is implemented to return the String in following form:

classname@hashcode in hexadecimal form.

Hence, the correct option is (D).

2. When an array is declared using new operator then all of its elements are initialized to 0 automatically. for loop body is executed 5 times as whenever controls comes in the loop i value is incremented twice, first by i++ in body of loop then by ++i in increment condition of for loop.

Output:

0 2 4 6 8 10 12 14 16 18

Hence, the correct option is (A).

3. Array arr contains 10 elements. n contains 6 thus in next line n is given value 3 printing arr[3]/2 i:e 3/2 = 1 because of int Value, by int values there is no rest. If this values would be float the result would be 1.5.

Output:

1

Hence, the correct option is (D).

4. The function __add__() is called first since it is within the bracket. The function __str__() is then called on the object that we received after adding A and B. Foo (pronounced Foo) is a term used by programmers as a placeholder for a value that can change, depending on conditions or on information passed to the program. It can be helpful to use metasyntactic variables when creating sample code because programmers don't have to create unique names for each variable value.

Hence, the correct option is (A).

5. This means C++ has the ability to provide the operators with a special meaning for a data type, this ability is known as operator overloading. For example, we can overload an operator '+' in a class like String so that we can concatenate two strings by just using +. So, __lg__() is invalid.

Hence, the correct option is (D).

6. C++ does not require struct keyword while declaring an object of the structure whereas in C we require struct tag for declaring an object. In C, we need to use struct to declare a struct variable. In C++, struct is not necessary.

For example, let there be a structure for Record. In C, we must use "struct Record" for Record variables. In C++, we need not use struct and using 'Record' only would work.

Hence, the correct option is (C).

7. C does not allow the programmer to declare any static members inside a class whether in C++ it is allowed to declare static variables. Static variables should not be declared inside structure.

The reason is C compiler requires the entire structure elements to be placed together (i.e.) memory allocation for structure members should be contiguous. Separating out one member alone to data segment defeats the purpose of static variable.

Hence, the correct option is (B).

8. # is the stringizing operator. It allows formal arguments within a macro definition to be converted to a string. The number-sign or "stringizing" operator (#) converts macro parameters to string literals without expanding the parameter definition. It's used only with macros that take arguments. Any white space between the tokens in the actual argument is reduced to a single white space in the resulting string literal.

The double-number-sign or token-pasting operator (##), which is sometimes called the merging or combining operator, is used in both object-like and function-like macros. It permits separate tokens to be joined into a single token, and therefore, can't be the first or last token in the macro definition.

<> is a relational operator.

% is an arithmetic operator.

Hence, the correct option is (B).

9. In this case, it is not necessary for the argument in the printf function to be enclosed in double quotes. However, if the argument is enclosed in double quotes, no error is thrown.

Output:

"56#7"

Hence, the correct option is (B).

10. The above code will result in an error. This is because we have passed to arguments to the macro hello, but it should be talking only one.

```
#include<stdio.h>

#define hello(c) #c

int main()
{
printf(hello("i,am"));

}
```

Output:

"i,am"

Hence, the correct option is (D).

11. As we have to declare an array of pointers of integers, therefore, we need double pointer array in which each element is collection pointers to integers. Therefore, the correct.

Syntax:

int **arr = new int*[10];

You can declare an array without a size specifier for the leftmost dimension in multiples cases: as a global variable with extern class storage (the array is defined elsewhere), as a function parameter: int main(int argc, char *argv[]). In this case, the size specified for the leftmost dimension is ignored anyway.

Hence, the correct option is (B).

12. All the statements about the new and malloc are correct. new is an operator whereas malloc() is a function. The constructor is called when new is used and new returns required type memory pointer.

malloc(): It is a C library function that can also be used in C++, while the "new" operator is specific for C++ only. Both malloc() and new are used to allocate the memory dynamically in heap. But "new" does call the constructor of a class whereas "malloc()" does not.

Hence, the correct option is (D).

13. In programming languages, ad hoc polymorphism is a kind of polymorphism in which polymorphic functions can be applied to arguments of different types, because a polymorphic function can denote a number of distinct and potentially heterogeneous implementations depending on the type of argument(s) to which it is applied. When applied to object-oriented or procedural concepts, it is also known as function overioading or operator overloading.

Hence, the correct option is (C).

14. Both statements are false because all the operators of C++ cannot be overloaded and the basic meaning of an operator cannot be changed, we can only give new meaning to an operator.

The = and & C++ operators are overloaded by default. For example, you can copy the objects of the same Class directly using the = operator.

Hence, the correct option is (D).

15. Hierarchical inheritance is used to make all the inherited classes have some common features obtained from a single base class. This allows all the classes to maintain a group or to be classified under one class.

For example, a car is a common class from which Audi, Ferrari, Maruti etc can be derived.

Hence, the correct option is (D).

16. Success callback function evoke only when User accepts to share location information. There is a privacy for sharing of user's location and the callback function is evoke only when a user accepts to share his location. Its input parameter is a position of the object. If this function fails then error callback function will be evoked.

Hence, the correct option is (A).

17. coords.latitude is the latitude in decimal number, coords.longitude is the value of longitude in decimal number, coords.altitude returns the value above mean sea level in meters if and only is return is available there. The accuracy attribute denotes the accuracy level of the latitude and longitude coordinates. It is specified in meters and must be supported by all implementations. The value of the accuracy attribute must be a non-negative real number. It's meters for PhoneGap, Google's various geo APIs, and so on.

Hence, the correct option is (D).

18. The value of timeout is positive long value. It specifies the maximum time in milliseconds which the user has taken to respond with the data of the location. Its default value is infinity.

Step to set the Window setTimeout():

- 1000 ms = 1 second.
- The function is only executed once. If you need to repeat execution, use the setInterval() method.
- Use the clearTimeout() method to prevent the function from running.

Hence, the correct option is (A).

19. To ensure that every event's response is generated after tasks are executed within their specified deadlines, the CPU and other core computation resources ought to be allocated to different tasks according to their priority levels. So, The task must not degrade over time.

Hence, the correct option is (B).

20. The technique in which the CPU generates physical addresses directly is known as Real addressing. Physical Address identifies a physical location of required data in memory. The user never directly deals with the physical address but can access by its corresponding logical address. The user program generates the logical address and thinks that the program is running in this logical address but the program needs physical memory for its execution, therefore, the logical address must be mapped to the physical address by MMU before they are used. The term Physical Address Space is used for all physical addresses corresponding to the logical addresses in a logical address space.

Hence, the correct option is (B).

21. This assumes that there is a very small probability that the actual size result will fall outside the optimistic or pessimistic values. PERT is a three point activity estimating technique that considers estimation uncertainty and risk by using three estimates to define an approximate probability for an activity's cost or duration.

The 3 points of estimates are as below:

- Optimistic estimate: Estimate when all favourable things will happen (all opportunities happen and no threats take place).
- Pessimistic estimate: Estimate when all unfavourable conditions happen (all threats happen and no opportunities take place).
- Most Likely estimate: Estimate.

Hence, the correct option is (B).

22. The three forms include the basic, intermediate and detailed COCOMO model. The first level, Basic COCOMO can be used for quick and slightly rough calculations of Software Costs. Its accuracy is somewhat restricted due to the absence of sufficient factor considerations.

Intermediate COCOMO takes these Cost Drivers into account and Detailed COCOMO additionally accounts for the influence of individual project phases, i.e in case of Detailed it accounts for both these cost drivers and also calculations are performed phase wise henceforth producing a more accurate result.

Hence, the correct option is (B).

23. Snapshot isolation is a particular type of Concurrency-control scheme. It has gained wide acceptance in commercial and open-source systems, including Oracle, PostgreSQL, and SQL Server.

In databases, and transaction processing (transaction management), snapshot isolation is a guarantee that all reads made in a transaction will see a consistent snapshot of the database (in practice it reads the last committed values that existed at the time it started), and the transaction itself will successfully commit only if no updates it has made conflict with any concurrent updates made since that snapshot.

Hence, the correct option is (A).

24. Under first updater wins the system uses a Locking mechanism that applies only to updates. Reads are unaffected by this since they do not obtain locks. The situation in which each pair of transactions has read data written by the other, but there is no data written by the transactions is called a write skew.

Hence, the correct option is (C).

25. Adding the for update clause causes the system to treat data that are read as if they had been updated for purposes of concurrency control. The FOR UPDATE clause is an optional part of a SELECT statement. Cursors are read-only by default. The FOR UPDATE clause specifies that the cursor should be updatable, and enforces a check during compilation that the SELECT statement meets the requirements for an updatable cursor.

Syntax:
FOR
{
READ ONLY | FETCH ONLY |
UPDATE [OF Simple-column-Name [, Simple-column-Name]*]
}

Hence, the correct option is (A).

26. A superkey is a combination of columns that uniquely identifies any row within a relational database management system (RDBMS) table. Functional dependencies (FD) are are type of constraint that is based on keys. A superkey is defined as in the relational schema R , where: a subset K of R is a subkey of R if, in any legal relation r(R), for all pairs, t1 and t2 in tuple r such that t1 is not equal to t2 then t1[K] is not equal to t2[K].

Hence, the correct option is (C).

27. The triggers run after an insert, update or delete on a table. They are not supported for views. A trigger is a special type of stored procedure that automatically runs when an event occurs in the database server. DML triggers run when a user tries to modify data through a data manipulation language (DML) event. DML events are INSERT, UPDATE or DELETE statements on a table or view.

Hence, the correct option is (B).

28. The revoke statement may specify restrict in order to prevent cascading revocation. The keyword cascade can be used instead of restrict to indicate that revocation should cascade. REVOKE DROPIN ON is used to revoke authorization to delete database objects in the specified schema from the user identified by grantee. REVOKE EXECUTE revokes the authorization to execute the database procedure or database function from the database user identified by grantee.

Hence, the correct option is (B).

29. The current role associated with a session can be set by executing set role name. The specified role must have been granted to the user, else the set role statement fails. Object privileges can be granted to and revoked from users and roles. If you grant object privileges to roles, you can make the privileges selectively available. Object privileges can be granted to or revoked from, users and roles using the SQL commands GRANT and REVOKE, respectively.

Hence, the correct option is (A).

30. Sequential control statements, which are not crucial to PL/SQL programming. The sequential control statements are GOTO, which goes to a specified statement, and NULL, which does nothing. PL/SQL has three categories of control statements: Conditional selection statements, which run different statements for different data values. The conditional selection statements are IF and CASE. Loop statements, which run the same statements with a series of different data values.

Hence, the correct option is (A).

31. Membership in a VLAN can be based on Port numbers, MAC address and IP address. A VLAN is a set of end stations and the switch ports that connect them.
Membership in a VLAN can be defined based on the ports that belong to the VLAN. For example, in a bridge with four ports, ports 1, 2, and 4 belong to VLAN 1 and port 3 belongs to VLAN 2.

Port	VLAN
1	1
2	1
3	2
4	1

Membership in a VLAN is based on the MAC address of the workstation. The switch tracks the MAC addresses which belong to each VLAN. Since MAC addresses form a part of the workstation's network interface card, when a workstation is moved, no reconfiguration is needed to allow the workstation to remain in the same VLAN. This is unlike Layer 1 VLAN's where membership tables must be reconfigured.

MAC Address	VLAN
1212354145121	1
2389234873743	2
3045834758445	2
5483573475843	1

VLAN membership for Layer 2 VLAN's can also be based on the protocol type field found in the Layer 2 header.

Protocol	VLAN

IP	1
IPX	2

Hence, the correct option is (D).

32. Configuration management can be divided into two subsystems: reconfiguration and Documentation. The documentation subsystem of configuration management handles the log making and reporting functions of the configuration management. It also reports the errors in the network caused by the configuration's failure.

Configuration management is a systems engineering process for establishing consistency of a product's attributes throughout its life. In the technology world, configuration management is an IT management process that tracks individual configuration items of an IT system.

IT systems are composed of IT assets that vary in granularity. An IT asset may represent a piece of software, or a server, or a cluster of servers. The following focuses on configuration management as it directly applies to IT software assets and software asset CI/CD.

Hence, the correct option is (A).

33. A packet-switched network is most preferred for pipelining process. Pipelining exponentially reduces the time taken to transmit a large number of packets in the network. An example of a circuit-switched network is an analog telephone network. It contrasts with packet-switched networks, which break the communication into packets and then send those packets through the network independently of one another. Message switching is still used for telegraph traffic and a modified form of it, known as packet switching, is used extensively for data communications.

Hence, the correct option is (C).

34. MIB is a collection of groups of objects that can be managed by SNMP. MIB stands for Management Information Base. Simple network management controls the group of objects in the management information base. It is usually used with SNMP (Simple Network Management Protocol). Simple Network Management Protocol (SNMP) is a networking protocol used for the management and monitoring of network-connected devices in Internet Protocol networks. It is an application layer protocol in the OSI model framework. Typically, the SNMP protocol is implemented using the User Datagram Protocol (UDP).

Hence, the correct option is (C).

35. SSH-2 does not contain Physical layer. SSH-2 is a more secure, portable and efficient version of SSH that includes SFTP, which is functionally similar to FTP, but is SSH-2 encrypted. On the main menu, click Tools > Global Options, or press ALT+F7. Expand the Security node, then click SSH-2 security. Select the Use public key authentication check box. In the Use Passphrase and Confirm passphrase boxes, type the passphrase for the key.

The physical layer defines the relationship between a device and a transmission medium, such as a copper or optical cable. This includes the layout of pins, voltages, cable specifications, hubs, repeaters, network adapters, host bus adapters (HBA used in storage area networks) and more.

Hence, the correct option is (C).

36. j = 41+1 =>42
k = 37-1 =>36
j = 42/36 =>1
k = 36/1 =>36

The correct code is:

```
#include <stdio.h>

int main()

{
int j=41,k= 37;
j=j+1;
k=k-1;
j=j/k;
k=k/j;
printf("%d %d",j,k);
}
```

Output:

1 36

Hence, the correct option is (D).

37. To solve this code, you need to have good understanding of ternary operator. (0 + 1 == 1) // True So, LHS becomes *(&b) // value at address of b. Now, a? b : c => 0?1:2 So, RHS leaves 2 On comparing, *(&b) = 2 or b =2. So, a=0, b=2, c=2.

Hence, the correct option is (C).

38. Let's track the program flow.

```
while (2<= 6)
{
k = 2*2 ->4
i = 2+1 ->3
}
while (3<= 6)
{
k = 4*3 ->12
i = 3+1 ->4
}
while (4<= 6)
{
k = 12*4 ->48
i = 4+1 ->5
}
while (5<= 6)
{
k = 48*5 ->240
i = 5+1 ->6
}
while (6<= 6)
{
k = 240*6 ->1440
i = 6+1 ->7
}
while(7<= 6) // false
Therefore, K = 1440.
```

Hence, the correct option is (C).

39. '<<' This is the left shift operator. It takes two numbers, left shifts the bits of the first operand, the second operand decides the number of places to shift. '>>' This is the right shift operator. 8 in binary form : 00001000 Performing Left Shift (<<) : 00010000 => 16 Performing Right Shift (>>) : 00000100 => 4.

Hence, the correct option is (C).

40. We need to find the address of Arr[17]. Starting base address is 1100.

Arr[1] – 1100 (2bytes)
Arr[2] – 1102 (2bytes)
Arr[3] – 1104 (2bytes)
Arr[4] – 1106 (2bytes)
Arr[5] – 1108 (2bytes)
Arr[6] – 1110 (2bytes)
Arr[7] – 1112 (2bytes)
Arr[8] – 1114 (2bytes)
Arr[9] – 1116 (2bytes)
Arr[10] – 1118 (2bytes)
Arr[11] – 1120 (2bytes)
Arr[12] – 1122 (2bytes)
Arr[13] – 1124 (2bytes)
Arr[14] – 1126 (2bytes)
Arr[15] – 1128 (2bytes)
Arr[16] – 1130 (2bytes)
Arr[17] – 1132 (2bytes)

Thus, the Answer for arr[17] is 1132.

Hence, the correct option is (A).

Mock Test 09

Q.1 What will be the output of the following pseudocode?

```
char x,y,z;
x='f';
y='s';
z='j';
int sum= x+y+z;
print(sum);
```

A. 320 **B.** 324 **C.** 323 **D.** 315

Q.2 What is output from the following code?

```
a = 2
loop while a< 10
print a + " "
a = a + 2
```

A. 2 4 6 8
B. 2 2 2
C. 2 4 6 8 10
D. 2 4 6

Q.3 What is output from the following code?

```
x = 10
loop while x >85
x = x - 5
print x
```

A. 5 **B.** 10 **C.** 80 **D.** 85

Q.4 What will be the output of the following pseudocode?

```
Integer x, y, z, a
Set x = 8, y = 6, z = 10
a = (x AND y) OR (z + 1)
Print a
```

A. 5 **B.** 3 **C.** 2 **D.** 1

Q.5 What will be the output of the following pseudocode for arr[]= 1,2,3,4,5,6,7,8,9,10?

```
initialize i,n
intialize and array of size n
accept the values for the array
for o to n
arr[i] = arr[i]+arr[i+1]
end for
print the array elements
```

A. 3 5 7 9 11 13 15 17 10
B. 3 5 7 9 11
C. 3 5 9 15 20
D. Error

Q.6 What will happen if in a C program you assign a value to an array element whose subscript exceeds the size of array?

A. The element will be set to 0.
B. The compiler would report an error.
C. The program may crash if some important data gets overwritten.
D. The array size would appropriately grow.

Q.7 In C, if you pass an array as an argument to a function, what actually gets passed?

A. Value of elements in array.
B. First element of the array.
C. Base address of the array.
D. Address of the last element of array.

Q.8 Which of the following statements mentioning the name of the array begins does not yield the base address?

A: When array name is used with the sizeof operator.
B: When array name is operand of the & operator.
C: When array name is passed to scanf() function.
D: When array name is passed to printf() function.

A. A **B.** A, B **C.** B **D.** B, D

Q.9 Which of the following statements are correct about an array?

1: The array int num[26]; can store 26 elements.
2: The expression num[1] designates the very first element in the array.
3: It is necessary to initialize the array at the time of declaration.
4: The declaration num[SIZE] is allowed if SIZE is a macro.

A. 1 **B.** 1, 4 **C.** 2, 3 **D.** 2, 4

Q.10 A function with the same name as the class, but preceded with a tilde character (~) is called ________ of that class.

A. Constructor
B. Destructor
C. Function
D. Object

Q.11 ________ used to make a copy of one class object from another class object of the same class type.

A. Constructor
B. Copy constructor
C. Destructor
D. Default constructor

Q.12 Which of the following correctly shows the hierarchy of arithmetic operations in C?

A. / + * - **B.** * - / + **C.** + - / * **D.** / * + -

Q.13 Which of the following is the correct usage of conditional operators used in C?

A. a>b?c=30:c=40
B. a>b?c=30
C. max = a>b?a>c?a:c:b>c?b:c
D. return (a>b)?(a:b)

Q.14 Which of the following is the correct order if calling functions in the below code?

a = f1(23, 14) * f2(12/4) + f3();

A. f1, f2, f3
B. f3, f2, f1
C. Order may vary from compiler to compiler.
D. None of above

Q.15 public class While

```
{
```

```
public void loop()
{
int x= 0;
while ( 1 ) /* Line 6 */
{
System.out.print("x plus one is " + (x + 1)); /* Line 8 */
}
}
}
```

Which statement is true?

A. There is a syntax error on line 1.
B. There are syntax errors on lines 1 and 6.
C. There are syntax errors on lines 1, 6, and 8.
D. There is a syntax error on line 6.

Q.16 Consider the following code fragment:

```
Rectangle r1 = new Rectangle();
r1.setColor(Color.blue);
Rectangle r2 = r1;
r2.setColor(Color.red);
```

After the above piece of code is executed, what are the colors of r1 and r2 (in this order)?

A. Color.blue Color.red
B. Color.blue Color.blue
C. Color.red Color.red
D. Color.red Color.blue

Q.17 The main function of scope resolution operator (::) is:

A. To define an object
B. To define a data member
C. To link the definition of an identifier to its declaration
D. All of the above

Q.18 A constructor initialization list produces similar results to:

A. Overriding
B. Assignment
C. Redeclaring
D. Output

Q.19 The most common operation used in constructors is:

A. Addition
B. Overloading
C. Assignment
D. Polymorphism

Q.20 For Cat and Animal class, correct way of inheritance is:

A. Class Cat: public Animal
B. Class Animal: public Cat
C. Both are correct way
D. None is correct way

Q.21 How many non-overlapping channels are available with 802.11h?

A. 3 **B.** 12 **C.** 23 **D.** 40

Q.22 A network management system can be divided into __________.

A. Three categories
B. Five broad categories
C. Seven broad categories
D. Ten broad categories

Q.23 Cisco's Unified Wireless Solution provides a mesh solution. What devices do you absolutely need to purchase to run a Cisco solution?

1. WCS
2. Controller
3. Access point
4. Bridge

A. 1 and 2
B. 2 and 3
C. 1 and 4 only
D. 4 only

Q.24 What is the maximum distance running the lowest data rate for 802.11b?

A. About 100 feet
B. About 175 feet
C. About 300 feet
D. About 350 feet

Q.25 What is the frequency range of the IEEE 802.11b standard?

A. 2.4Gbps **B.** 5Gbps **C.** 2.4GHz **D.** 5GHz

Q.26 Some advantages of the database approach include all, but:

A. Minimal data redundancy
B. Improved data consistency
C. Improved data sharing
D. Program-data dependency

Q.27 Structured data may include which of the following?

A. Photo image
B. Video clip
C. Dates
D. None of the above

Q.28 The separation of the data definition from the program is known as:

A. Data dictionary
B. Data independence
C. Data integrity
D. Referential integrity

Q.29 The Enterprise tier of the three-tiered database architecture includes:

A. Managing the data
B. Managing the User-system interface
C. Processing HTTP protocol
D. Processing scripting tasks

Q.30 The database design that consists of multiple tables that are linked together through matching data stored in each table is called:

A. Hierarchical database
B. Network database
C. Object oriented database
D. Relational database

Q.31 Which of the following is aggregate function in SQL?

A. AVG
B. SELECT
C. DISTINCT
D. None of the above

Q.32 Given relations R(w,x) and S(y,z), the result of:

```
SELECT DISTINCT w, x
FROM R, S
```

Is guaranteed to be same as R, if:

A. R has no duplicates and S is non-empty.

B. R and S have no duplicates.
C. S has no duplicates and R is non-empty.
D. R and S have the same number of tuples.

Q.33 Which internal exception is raised when a program references a nested table or varray element using an index number larger than the number of elements in the collection.
A. NO_DATA_FOUND
B. COLLECTION_IS_NULL
C. SUBSCRIPT_OUTSIDE_LIMIT
D. SUBSCRIPT_BEYOND_COUNT

Q.34 External command is DOS are:
A. Sys, ver, vol
B. Chkdsk, prompt, date
C. Edit, sys, chkdsk
D. Copy, edit, sys, format

Q.35 If you need to duplicate the entire disk, which command will you use?
A. Format
B. Diskcopy
C. Chkdsk
D. Copy

Q.36 To start a list using circles, use:
A. <ul "round">
B. <ul type="circle">
C. <ul type="round">
D. <ul ="round">

Q.37 The tag which allows some Web server search engines to search your Web page:
A. <search>
B. <isindex>
C. <head>
D. <link>

Q.38 If you create an HTML page in word processor:
A. Save it with binary file
B. Save it with WMF file
C. Save it with ASCII text file
D. All of the above

Q.39 A documented life cycle model helps to identify______________ in development process.
A. Inconsistencies
B. Redundancies
C. Commission
D. All of the above

Q.40 Irrespective of the model followed to develop a software product, the final document is written to reflect.
A. Iterative model
B. Classical waterfall model
C. Prototype model
D. Evolutionary model

// Smart Answer Sheet //

Correct Indicates percentage of students who answered questions correctly.

Skipped Indicates percentage of students who skipped questions.

Q.	Ans.	Correct	Skipped
1	C	62.47 %	1.12 %
2	A	49.49 %	1.07 %
3	B	25.79 %	4.83 %
4	D	22.18 %	3.55 %
5	A	47.6 %	1.99 %
6	C	58.14 %	1.98 %
7	C	62.24 %	1.13 %
8	B	43.4 %	1.09 %
9	B	82.69 %	0.0 %
10	B	82.32 %	0.0 %
11	B	63.66 %	1.98 %
12	D	49.18 %	1.12 %
13	C	22.48 %	3.25 %
14	C	60.76 %	1.35 %
15	D	17.28 %	4.6 %
16	C	49.76 %	1.62 %
17	B	52.44 %	1.65 %
18	B	77.85 %	0.0 %
19	C	78.85 %	0.0 %
20	A	68.75 %	1.1 %
21	C	41.6 %	1.33 %
22	B	78.66 %	0.0 %
23	B	17.81 %	3.53 %
24	D	26.92 %	3.36 %
25	C	44.23 %	1.11 %
26	D	65.1 %	1.51 %
27	C	78.2 %	0.0 %
28	B	53.35 %	1.71 %
29	A	46.05 %	1.72 %
30	D	64.51 %	1.8 %
31	A	78.05 %	0.0 %
32	A	60.91 %	1.41 %
33	D	27.76 %	3.25 %
34	C	56.1 %	2.0 %
35	B	65.15 %	1.78 %
36	B	45.86 %	1.37 %
37	B	47.55 %	1.71 %
38	A	53.64 %	1.25 %
39	D	78.42 %	0.0 %
40	B	47.61 %	1.86 %

Performance Analysis	
Avg. Score (%)	65.0%
Toppers Score (%)	70.0%
Your Score	

//Hints and Solutions//

1. The correct code is-

```
#include <stdio.h>
int main()
{
char x,y,z;
x='f';
y='s';
z='j';
int sum= x+y+z;
printf("%d",sum);
return 0;
}
```

Output:

323

Hence, the correct option is (C).

2. The correct code is-

```
#include<stdio.h>
int main()
{
int a = 2;
while (a<10)
{
printf("%d",a);
a = a + 2;
}
return 0;
}
```

Output:

2 4 6 8

Hence, the correct option is (A).

3. The correct code is-

```
#include<stdio.h>
int main()
{
int X = 10;
while (X>85)
{
X = X - 5;
}
printf("%d",X);
return 0;
}
```

Output:

10

Hence, the correct option is (B).

4. AND operator works when both the conditions are true so the first (x and y) condition will be taken as true as both the inputs are true. OR operator works when any of the conditions are true, where it has already got one of its input as true so without checking the other input it will directly assign the value as 1.

The correct code is-

```
#include<stdio.h>
int main()
{
int x=8,y=6,z=10,a;
a=(x&&y)||(z+1);
printf("%d",a);
return 0;
}
```

Output:

1

Hence, the correct option is (D).

5. The following pseudocode will add the first element with the second, the second element with the third, the third element with the fourth and the fourth element with the fifth, the fifth element will remain as it is.

So, the output is-

3 5 7 9 11 13 15 17 10

Hence, the correct option is (A).

6. If the index of the array size is exceeded, the program will crash. But the modern compilers will take care of this kind of errors.

Example: Run the below program, it will crash in Windows (TurboC Compiler).

```
#include<stdio.h>
int main()
{
int arr[2];
arr[3]=10;
printf("%d",arr[3]);
return 0;
}
```

Hence, the correct option is (C).

7. When we pass an array as a function argument, the base address of the array will be passed.

```
int* pc, c;
c = 5;
pc = &c;
*pc = 1;
printf("%d", *pc); // Ouptut: 1
printf("%d", c); // Output: 1
```

Hence, the correct option is (C).

8. Statement A and B does not yield the base address of the array. While the scanf() and printf() yields the base address of the array. No, mentioning the array name in C or C++ gives the base address in all contexts except one. The base address of an array is the address value of the starting point of the array. It is usually the address of the first element of the array. The base address can be used to calculate the other values of the array if width of the array and all info is given.

Hence, the correct option is (B).

9. 1. The array int num[26]; can store 26 elements. This statement is true.

2. The expression num[1] designates the very first element in the array. This statement is false, because it designates the second element of the array.

3. It is necessary to initialize the array at the time of declaration. This statement is false.

4. The declaration num[SIZE] is allowed if SIZE is a macro. This statement is true, because the macro just replaces the symbol SIZE with given value.

Hence, the correct option is (B).

10. A destructor is a member function that is invoked automatically when the object goes out of scope or is explicitly destroyed by a call to delete. A destructor has the same name as the class, preceded by a tilde (~).

Hence, the correct option is (B).

11. Copy constructor used to make a copy of one class object from another class object of the same class type. The copy constructor is a constructor which creates an object by initializing it with an object of the same class, which has been created previously. The copy constructor is used to-Initialize one object from another of the same type. Copy an object to pass it as an argument to a function.

For example, Student s1=s2, where, Student is the class. When the object of the same class type is passed by value as an argument.

Hence, the correct option is (B).

12. Simply called as BODMAS (Bracket of Division, Multiplication, Addition and Subtraction).

How Do I Remember? BODMAS!

- B - Brackets first.
- O - Orders (ie Powers and Square Roots, etc).
- DM - Division and Multiplication (left-to-right).
- AS - Addition and Subtraction (left-to-right).

Hence, the correct option is (D).

13. Option (A): assignment statements are always return in paranthesis in the case of conditional operator. It should be a>b?(c=30):(c=40).

Option (B): it is syntatically wrong.

Option (D): syntatically wrong, it should be return(a>b?a:b).

Option (C): it uses nested conditional operator, this is logic for finding greatest number out of three numbers.

Hence, the correct option is (C).

14. Here, multiplication will happen before the addition, but in which order the functions would be called is undefined. In an arithmetic expression, the parenthesis tell the compiler which operands go with which operators but do not force the compiler to evaluate everything within the parenthesis first.

Hence, the correct option is (C).

15. Using the integer 1 in the while statement, or any other looping or conditional construct for that matter will result in a syntax error on line 6. This is old C++ Program syntax, not valid Java. (A), (B) and (C) are incorrect because line 1 is valid (Java is case sensitive. So, While is a valid class name). Line 8 is also valid because an equation may be placed in a string operation as shown.

Hence, the correct option is (D).

16. Both r1 and r2 are referring the same object of Rectangle class. So, finally the Color of the object is changed to red.

- Object: Objects have states and behaviors. An object is an instance of a class. Object is r1 and r2.
- Class: A class can be defined as a template/blueprint that describes the behavior/state that the object of its type support. Class is Rectangle.

So, the output is:

Color.red
Color.red

Hence, the correct option is (C).

17. The scope resolution operator (::) is used for several reasons. The main function of scope resolution operator (::) is to define a data member. For example: If the global variable name is same as local variable name, the scope resolution operator will be used to call the global variable. It is also used to define a function outside the class and used to access the static variables of class.

Hence, the correct option is (B).

18. Example:

```
class test1
{
private:
int a;
int b;
public:
test1():a(0),b(0){}
};
class test2
{
private:
int a;
int b;
public:
test2()
```

```
{
a=0;
b=0;
}
};
```

Now, I know that test1() constructor is the right way to initialize the data members of a class because in test2() we are performing assignment and not initialization.

Hence, the correct option is (B).

19. The most common operation used in constructors is assignment. Assignment operators are used to assigning value to a variable. The left side operand of the assignment operator is a variable and right side operand of the assignment operator is a value. The example of assignment operator are "=", "+=", "-=", "*=", "/=".

Hence, the correct option is (C).

20. Firstly, keyword class should come, followed by the derived class name. Colon is must followed by access in which base class has to be derived, followed by the base class name. Inheritance in java is one of the core concepts of Object-Oriented Programming. Java Inheritance is used when we have is-a relationship between objects. Inheritance in Java is implemented using extends keyword.

Hence, the correct option is (A).

21. The IEEE 802.11h standard provides an addition 11 channels to the 802.11a standard's 12 non-overlapping channel for a total of 23 non-overlapping channels. Each channel on the 2.4 GHz spectrum is 20 MHz wide. The channel centers are separated by 5 MHz, and the entire spectrum is only 100 MHz wide. This means the 11 channels have to squeeze into the 100 MHz available, and in the end, overlap.

Hence, the correct option is (C).

22. The five broad categories of network management are:

- **Fault Management:** Fault management, in many ways, is the most fundamental area of the ISO network management model because it addresses the ability to maintain operations of the entire infrastructure.
- **Configuration Management:** Configuration management involves more than just the initial setup of routers, switches, servers or other pieces of network equipment. It also encompasses the ongoing tracking of any changes to the configuration of the system.
- **Accounting Management:** Accounting management documents all network utilization information. Primarily for bookkeeping purposes, accounting management will bill back or track departments or lines of business for usage.
- **Performance Management:** Performance management aims to ensure acceptable service levels in the network to support optimal business operations. A big component of performance management is collecting statistics on network service quality on an ongoing and consistent basis.
- **Security Management:** Security management is a multilayered discipline within network management that requires ongoing collection and analysis of relevant information. Functions that fall under the security management umbrella include network authentication, authorization and auditing.

Hence, the correct option is (B).

23. The Cisco Unified Wireless Solution is a great product, but you must purchase specialized devices. Cisco managed access points and a controller are the devices you need to purchase to run the Unified Wireless Solution.

Hence, the correct option is (B).

24. The IEEE 802.11b standard provides the lowest data rate at 1Mbps, but it also has the longest distance, which is about 350 feet.

Maximum distance running: Typical long-distance track races range from 3000 meters (1.87 miles) to 10,000 meters (6.2 miles), cross country races usually cover 5 to 12 km (3 to 7½ miles), while road races can be significantly longer, reaching 100 km (62 mi) and beyond.

Hence, the correct option is (D).

25. The IEEE 802.11b and IEEE 802.11g standards both run in the 2.4GHz RF range. The 802.11 standard provides a maximum theoretical 11 Megabits per second (Mbps) data rate in the 2.4 GHz Industrial, Scientific and Medical (ISM) band.

Hence, the correct option is (C).

26. Advantage of the database is not program-data dependency. Program-data independence refers to the capability of leaving data intact and accessible regardless of modifications to the database that contains the data.

- The file based data management systems contained multiple files that were stored in many different locations in a system or even across multiple systems. Because of this, there were sometimes multiple copies of the same file which lead to data redundancy.
- This is prevented in a database as there is a single database and any change in it is reflected immediately. Because of this, there is no chance of encountering duplicate data.
- Data consistency is ensured in a database because there is no data redundancy. All data appears consistently across the database and the data is same for all the users viewing the database. Moreover, any changes made to the database are immediately reflected to all the users and there is no data inconsistency.
- In a database, the users of the database can share the data among themselves. There are various levels of authorisation to access the data, and consequently, the data can only be shared based on the correct authorisation protocols being followed.

- Many remote users can also access the database simultaneously and share the data between themselves.

Hence, the correct option is (D).

27. The term structured data generally refers to data that has a defined length and format for big data. Examples of structured data include numbers, dates, and groups of words and numbers called strings. Most experts agree that this kind of data accounts for about 20 percent of the data that is out there. Structured data is the data you're probably used to dealing with. It's usually stored in a database.

Hence, the correct option is (C).

28. Data Independence is defined as a property of DBMS that helps you to change the Database schema at one level of a database system without requiring to change the schema at the next higher level. Data independence helps you to keep data separated from all programs that make use of it.

Hence, the correct option is (B).

29. Three-tiered database architecture is a well-established software application architecture that organizes applications into three logical and physical computing tiers: the presentation tier, or user interface; the application tier, where data is processed; and the data tier, where the data associated with the application is stored and managed.

Hence, the correct option is (A).

30. A relational database is a collection of data items organized as a set of formally described tables from which data can be accessed or reassembled. A relational database management system is a simpler database model, both to design and implement.

Hence, the correct option is (D).

31. AVG is one of the aggregate functions. It returns average value after calculating from values in a numeric column.

Syntax:

SELECT AVG(column_name) FROM table_name;

Hence, the correct option is (A).

32. The query selects all attributes of R. Since we have distinct in query, result can be equal to R only if R doesn't have duplicates. If we do not give any attribute on which we want to join two tables, then the queries like above become equivalent to Cartesian product. Cartesian product of two sets will be empty if any of the two sets is empty. So, S should have atleast one record to get all rows of R.

Hence, the correct option is (A).

33. SUBSCRIPT_BEYOND_COUNT References a nested table or varray element using an index number larger than the number of elements in the collection. The SUBSCRIPT_BEYOND_COUNT error is where the in-limit of a subscript was greater than that of the count of a varray or was too large for a nested table. When an error occurs, an internal exception is raised. Error is a bug whereas internal exception is a warning or an error condition. Internal exception are handled, but errors are not.

Hence, the correct option is (D).

34. External command is DOS are edit, sys, chkdsk. An external command is an DOS command that is not included in command.com. External commands are commonly external either because they require large requirements or are not commonly used commands. It requires a separate file to operate. Fdisk is an external command that only works if fdisk.exe, or in some cases, fdisk.com, is present.

External commands:

defrag.exe
edit.com
fdisk.exe
scandisk.exe

Hence, the correct option is (C).

35. Diskcopy command is used only for copying diskettes, not fixed disks. Diskcopy checks to determine if the disk in the target drive has been previously formatted. If not, Diskcopy will format it before it starts the copy (except in early versions of DOS). If the target drive is the same as the source drive (or if you do not enter a drive designator), the copying will be done using one drive.

Hence, the correct option is (B).

36. To start a list using circles, use <ul type="circle">. circle is a type of unordered list. it gives a bulletin format.

Example:

```
<!DOCTYPE html>
<html>
<body>
<ul type="circle">
<li>HTML</li>
<li>Java</li>
<li>JavaScript</li>
<li>SQL</li>
</ul>
</body>
</html>
```

Output:

- HTML
- Java
- JavaScript
- SQL

Hence, the correct option is (B).

37. HTML <isindex> tag is used to provide a single line text input in a page to query a document. If user sent input to the server then server returns the list of page matching with the query. The <isindex> tag can be used anywhere in the document, but it would be preferable to use it within <head> tag.

Syntax:

<isindex prompt = "Search your document here" />

Hence, the correct option is (B).

38. If you create an HTML page in word processor save it with binary file. There are different types of saving format available based on their type like for textural data you must use the ASCII format, but in case of the HTML file you need to use the Binary format for saving the file as it is coding. Because in binary files they save both text and codes both.

Hence, the correct option is (A).

39. A documented life cycle model helps to identify inconsistencies, redundancies and ommission in development process. It is a technique that produces software with the highest caliber and least expensive within the shortest possible time. SDLC provides a well-structured flow of stages that assist a company to quickly produce high-quality software that is well-examined and ready for production use.

Hence, the correct option is (D).

40. Irrespective of the model followed to develop a software product, the final document is written to reflect in classical waterfall model. It is an idealistic model for software development. This model is very simple and is easy to understand. Phases in this model are processed one at a time. Each stage in the model is clearly defined. This model has very clear and well undestood milestones. Process, actions and results are very well documented. Reinforces good habits: define-before- design, design-before-code. This model works well for smaller projects and projects where requirements are well understood.

Hence, the correct option is (B).

Mock Test 10

Q.1 What would be the output of the following code snippet if variable a=10?

```
if(a<=0)
{
if(a==0)
{
System.out.println("1 ");
}
else
{
System.out.println("2 ");
}
}
System.out.println("3 ");
```

A. 1 2 **B.** 2 3 **C.** 1 3 **D.** 3

Q.2 What will be the output of the following Java program?

```
int var1 = 5;
int var2 = 6;
if ((var2 = 1) == var1)
System.out.print(var2);
else
System.out.print(+var2);
```

A. 1 **B.** 2 **C.** 3 **D.** 4

Q.3 What will be the output of the following Java program?

```
int sum = 0;
for (int i = 0, j = 0; i< 5 & j< 5; ++i, j = i + 1)
sum += i;
System.out.println(sum);
```

A. 5 **B.** 6
C. 14 **D.** Compilation error

Q.4 What will be the output of the following Java program?

```
int a = 5;
int b = 10;
first:
{
second:
{
third:
{
if (a == b >>1)
break second;
}
print a;
}
print b;
}
```

A. 5 10 **B.** 10 5 **C.** 5 **D.** 10

Q.5 In the follwing code 3553 is giving as a input then, what is final output?

```
printf("Enter an integer \n");
scanf("%d", &num);
/* original number is stored at temp */
temp = num;
while (num >0)
{
remainder = num % 10;
reverse = reverse * 10 + remainder;
num /= 10;
}
printf("Given number is = %d\n", temp);
printf("Its reverse is = %d\n", reverse);
if (temp == reverse)
printf("Number is a palindrome \n");
else
printf("Number is not a palindrome \n");
```

A. Given number is palindrome
B. Given number is not a palindrome
C. 10
D. None of the above

Q.6 Study the following program:

```
main ()
{
char x;
x = 'A' + 5;
printf("%c", x);
}
```

What will be the output of this program?

A. A + 5 **B.** A **C.** 5 **D.** F

Q.7 Study the following program:

```
#include<stdio.h>
#define a( i, j ) printf("%d", j##i )
int main()
{
a(5, 10);
}
```

What will be the output of this program?

A. 510 **B.** 105
C. 150 **D.** Compiler error

Q.8 Which of the following initialization is incorrect in C language?

A. char str [40] = "YUGAL";
B. char str [] = {'Y','U','G','A','L','\ 0'};
C. char str [40] = {'Y','U','G','A','L','\ 0'};
D. None of the these

Q.9 What will be the output of the following C code?

```
#define display(text) printf(#text "@")
main()
{
display(hello.);
display(good morning!);
}
```

A. hello.@good morning!
B. error
C. hello.good morning!@
D. hello.@good morning!@

Q.10 What will be the output of the following C code?

```
#define hello(c,d) #c #d
main()
{
printf(hello(i,"am"));
}
```

A. iam **B.** i"am" **C.** am **D.** "am"

Q.11 What will happen when we move the try block far away from catch block?

A. Reduces the amount of code in the cache.
B. Increases the amount of code in the cache.
C. Don't alter anything.
D. Increases the amount of code.

Q.12 What will be the output of the following C++ code?

```
#include<iostream>
using namespace std;
class A
{
~A(){
cout<<"Destructor called\n";
}
};
int main()
{
A a;
return 0;
}
```

A. Destructor called
B. Nothing will be printed
C. Error
D. Segmentation fault

Q.13 What will be the output of the following C++ code?

```
#include<iostream>
using namespace std;
class A
{
~A(){
cout<<"Destructor called\n";
}
};
int main()
{
A *a1 = new A();
A *a2 = new A();
return 0;
}
```

A. Destructor called
B. Destructor called
Destructor called
C. Error
D. Nothing is printed

Q.14 What will be the output of the following Java code?

```
class multidimention_array
{
public static void main(String args[])
{
int arr[][] = new int[3][];
arr[0] = new int[1];
arr[1] = new int[2];
arr[2] = new int[3];
int sum = 0;
for (int i = 0; i< 3; ++i)
for (int j = 0; j< i + 1; ++j)
arr[i][j] = j + 1;
for (int i = 0; i< 3; ++i)
for (int j = 0; j< i + 1; ++j)
sum = sum + arr[i][j];
System.out.print(sum);
}
}
```

A. 11 **B.** 10 **C.** 13 **D.** 14

Q.15 What will be the output of the following Java code?

```
class array_output
{
public static void main(String args[])
{
char array_variable [] = new char[10];
for (int i = 0; i< 10; ++i)
{
array_variable[i] = 'i';
System.out.print(array_variable[i] + "");
}
}
}
```

A. 1 2 3 4 5 6 7 8 9 10
B. 0 1 2 3 4 5 6 7 8 9 10
C. i j k l m n o p q r
D. i i i i i i i i i i

Q.16 Which of the following is correct about new and malloc?

A. Both are available in C.
B. Pointer object initialization of a class with both new and malloc calls the constructor of that class.
C. Pointer object initialization of a class using new involves constructor call whereas using malloc does not involve constructor call.
D. Pointer object initialization of a class using malloc involves constructor call whereas using new does not involve constructor call.

Q.17 What is virtual inheritance?

A. C++ technique to avoid multiple copies of the base class into children/derived class.
B. C++ technique to avoid multiple inheritances of classes.
C. C++ technique to enhance multiple inheritance.
D. C++ technique to ensure that a private member of the base class can be accessed somehow.

Q.18 What is the difference between delete and delete[] in C++?

A. Delete is used to delete normal objects whereas delete[] is used to pointer object.

B. Delete is a keyword whereas delete[] is an identifier.

C. Delete is used to delete single object whereas delete[] is used to multiple (array/pointer of) objects.

D. Delete is syntactically correct but delete[] is wrong and so will give an error if used in any case.

Q.19 Which of the following is an exit-controlled loop?

A. For

B. While

C. Do-while

D. All of the mentioned

Q.20 Which of the following is an entry-controlled loop?

A. For **B.** While

C. Do-while **D.** Both while and for

Q.21 Which property is like the GPS in car?

A. watchPosition()

B. clearWatch()

C. getCurrentPosition()

D. showPosition()

Q.22 Which is not the case of invoking for error callback function?

A. User denies to share the information of a location

B. Location information is unavailable

C. Request timed out

D. When we are using wi-fi

Q.23 Maximum age returns time in ___________.

A. Nano-seconds **B.** Milli-seconds

C. Hour **D.** Seconds

Q.24 The delay that occur during the playback of a stream is called __________.

A. Stream delay **B.** Playback delay

C. Jitter **D.** Event delay

Q.25 Which algorithm can be optimized to meet the timing deadlines and rate requirements of continuous media?

A. Earliest-Deadline-First scheduling

B. SCAN-EDF scheduling

C. Both (A) and (B)

D. None of the mentioned

Q.26 Which of the following is not one of the five information domain characteristics of Function Point (FP) decomposition?

A. External inputs **B.** External outputs

C. External process **D.** External inquiries

Q.27 If an Indirect approach is taken, then the sizing approach is represented as:

A. LOC **B.** FP

C. Fuzzy Logic **D.** LOC and FP

Q.28 Identify the DBMS among the following?

A. PL/SQL **B.** MS-PowerPoin

C. MS-Access **D.** MS-Excel

Q.29 Facebook Tackles Big Data With ______ based on Hadoop.

A. 'Project Prism' **B.** 'Prism'

C. 'Project Big' **D.** 'Project Data'

Q.30 Find out the wrong statement:

A. If V2 and V3 are the same, you only need to use setOutputValueClass().

B. The overall effect of Streaming job is to perform a sort of the input.

C. A Streaming application can control the separator that is used when a key-value pair is turned into a series of bytes and sent to the map or reduce process over standard input.

D. None of the mentioned

Q.31 Which of the following is a NoSQL Database Type?

A. SQL

B. Document databases

C. JSON

D. All of the mentioned

Q.32 Which of the following is a wide-column store?

A. Cassandra **B.** Riak

C. MongoDB **D.** Redis

Q.33 Which of the following is used to access the database server at the time of executing the program and get the data from the server accordingly?

A. Embedded SQL **B.** Dynamic SQL

C. SQL declarations **D.** SQL data analysis

Q.34 Which of the following function is used to find the column count of the particular resultset?

A. getMetaData() **B.** Metadata()

C. getColumn() **D.** get Count()

Q.35 What is a \%ROWTYPE attribute used for?

A. To declare a record variable that represents a full or partial row of a database table.

B. To declare a record variable that represents a full row of a database table only.

C. To declare a record variable that represents a partial row of a database table only.

D. To declare a record variable from another record variable.

Q.36 Users use often __________ for access to mainframe or super computer.

A. Terminal **B.** Node

C. Desktop **D.** Hand held

Q.37 Determine the maximum length of the cable (in km) for transmitting data at a rate of 500 Mbps in an Ethernet LAN with frames of size 10000 bits. Assume the signal speed in the cable to be 2,00,000 km/s.

A. 1 km **B.** 2 km **C.** 2.5 km **D.** 6 km

Q.38 What is used to identify whether a data word has an odd or even number of 1's?

A. Cary bit **B.** Zero bit

C. Parity bit **D.** Sign bit

Q.39 A combination of hardware and software, which provides facilities sending and rationing of information between computer devices is called a:

A. Network
B. Peripheral
C. Expansion slot
D. Digital device

Q.40 Server is a computer which provides resources to other computers commuted in a _________.

A. Network
B. Mainframe
C. Super computers
D. Clients

// Smart Answer Sheet //

Correct Indicates percentage of students who answered questions correctly.

Skipped Indicates percentage of students who skipped questions.

Q.	Ans.	Correct	Skipped
1	D	54.88 %	1.54 %
2	B	42.45 %	1.27 %
3	B	80.61 %	0.0 %
4	D	62.91 %	1.98 %
5	A	28.26 %	3.12 %
6	D	50.71 %	1.46 %
7	B	30.6 %	4.26 %
8	D	85.48 %	0.0 %

Q.	Ans.	Correct	Skipped
9	D	66.48 %	1.12 %
10	B	82.92 %	0.0 %
11	A	64.23 %	1.16 %
12	C	18.89 %	4.59 %
13	D	43.58 %	1.53 %
14	B	11.78 %	4.49 %
15	D	14.9 %	3.81 %
16	C	68.11 %	1.06 %

Q.	Ans.	Correct	Skipped
17	A	80.96 %	0.0 %
18	C	40.53 %	1.93 %
19	C	69.27 %	1.26 %
20	D	53.14 %	1.36 %
21	A	47.91 %	1.11 %
22	D	62.66 %	1.97 %
23	B	44.03 %	1.79 %
24	C	32.53 %	3.02 %

Q.	Ans.	Correct	Skipped
25	C	61.29 %	1.7 %
26	C	65.88 %	1.78 %
27	B	65.41 %	1.94 %
28	C	84.1 %	0.0 %
29	A	44.11 %	1.77 %
30	D	11.55 %	4.39 %
31	B	54.64 %	1.53 %
32	A	55.81 %	1.63 %

Q.	Ans.	Correct	Skipped
33	B	49.08 %	1.4 %
34	A	22.99 %	4.71 %
35	A	78.63 %	0.0 %
36	A	46.34 %	1.93 %
37	B	18.84 %	4.52 %
38	C	43.22 %	1.12 %
39	A	86.03 %	0.0 %
40	A	44.38 %	1.28 %

Performance Analysis	
Avg. Score (%)	47.5%
Toppers Score (%)	67.5%
Your Score	

//Hints and Solutions//

1. Since the first if condition is not met, control would not go inside if statement and hence only statement after the entire if block will be executed. These two conditions of if statements are false in the given following code:

```
if(a<=0)

{

if(a==0)

{
```

10<=0 False

10==0 False

Therefore, the else condition will run.

So, the output is 3.

Hence, the correct option is (D).

2. var2 is initialised to 1. The conditional statement returns false and the else part gets executed.

```
class selection_statements
{
public static void main(String args[])
{
int var1 = 5;
int var2 = 6;
if ((var2 = 1) == var1)
System.out.print(var2);
else
System.out.print(++var2);
}
}
```

Output:

2

Hence, the correct option is (B).

3. Using comma operator, we can include more than one statement in the initialization and iteration portion of the for loop. Therefore, both ++i and j = i + 1 is executed i gets the value – 0,1,2,3,4 & j gets the values -0,1,2,3,4,5.

```
class comma_operator
{
public static void main(String args[])
{
int sum = 0;
for (int i = 0, j = 0; i< 5 & j< 5; ++i, j = i + 1)
sum += i;
System.out.println(sum);
}
}
```

Output:

6

Hence, the correct option is (B).

4. b >> 1 in if returns 5 which is equal to a i:e 5, therefore, body of if is executed and block second is exited. Control goes to end of the block second executing the last print statement, printing 10.

```
class Output
{
public static void main(String args[])
{
int a = 5;
int b = 10;
first:
{
second:
{
third:
{
if (a == b >>1)
break second;
}
System.out.println(a);
}
System.out.println(b);
}
}
}
```

Output:

10

Hence, the correct option is (D).

5.
```
#include<stdio.h>

void main()
{
int num, temp, remainder, reverse = 0;
printf("Enter an integer \n");
scanf("%d", &num);
/* original number is stored at temp */
temp = num;
while (num >0)
{
remainder = num % 10;
reverse = reverse * 10 + remainder;
num /= 10;
}
printf("Given number is = %d\n", temp);
printf("Its reverse is = %d\n", reverse);
if (temp == reverse)
printf("Number is a palindrome \n");
else
printf("Number is not a palindrome \n");
}
```

Output:

Enter an integer
3553
Given number is = 3553
Its reverse is = 3553
Number is a palindrome.

Hence, the correct option is (A).

6. This program will print F because capital 'A' is equal to 65 according to the ASCII table. Therefore, 'A + 5' is equal to 70, and the value of 70 is F. ASCII stands for American Standard Code for Information Interchange. ASCII character table, including descriptions of the first 32 characters. ASCII was originally designed for use with teletypes, and so the descriptions are somewhat obscure and their use is frequently not as intended.

Hence, the correct option is (D).

7. The following program will execute by the given arguments i.e. a(i, j) = a(5,10). Therefore, it will print the output by the given print statement that is, printf("%d", j##i). In the print statement, it states that then it will print the output as that first it will print the value of j then the value of i which is already defined in arguments. So, the output is:

105

Hence, the correct option is (B).

8. All these declarations are correct in the C language. Initialization is the assignment of an initial value for a data object or variable. The manner in which initialization is performed depends on the programming language, as well as the type, storage class, etc., of an object to be initialized. Programming constructs that perform initialization are typically called initializers and initializer lists. Initialization is distinct from (and preceded by) declaration, although the two can sometimes be conflated in practice. The complement of initialization is finalization, which is primarily used for objects, but not variables.

Hence, the correct option is (D).

9. Each actual argument is converted into string within the printf function. Each argument is concatenated with '@', which is written as a separate string within the macro definition.

Output:

hello.@good morning!@

Hence, the correct option is (D).

10. The output for the following C code will be i"am". Since 2 arguments are passed and the macro hello takes two arguments, there is no error. An argument is referred to the values that are passed within a function when the function is called. These values are generally the source of the function that requires the arguments during the process of execution. These values are assigned to the variables in the definition of the function that is called.

Hence, the correct option is (B).

11. Compilers may try to move the catch-code far away from the try-code, which reduces the amount of code to keep in the cache, thus it will enhance the overall performance. While during dynamic memory allocation, our system may not have sufficient resources to handle it. So it is better to use it inside the try block. The code which can throw any exception is kept inside(or enclosed in) a try block. Then, when the code will lead to any error, that error/exception will get caught inside the catch block.

Hence, the correct option is (A).

12. Whenever a destructor is private then one should not define any normal object as it will be destroyed at the end of the program which will call destructor and as destructor is private the program gives error during compile while in case of pointer object the compiler at compile does not know about the object, therefore, does not gives compile error. So, when the destructor is private then the programmer can declare pointer object but cannot declare a normal object.

Hence, the correct option is (C).

13. The pointer object is created is not deleted so, the destructor for these objects is not called therefore nothing is printed on the screen. A pointer is a type of variable that carries location information. In this case, the example variable will store the address of an Order object that we want to interact with. We initialize the pointer variable by using the C++ new operator to construct a new object of type Order.

Hence, the correct option is (D).

14. arr[][] is a 2D array, the array has been allotted memory in parts. 1st row contains 1 element, 2nd row contains 2 elements and 3rd row contains 3 elements. each element of the array is given i + j value in the loop. Sum contains addition of all the elements of the array.

Output:

```
javac multidimention_array.java
java multidimention_array
10
```

Hence, the correct option is (B).

15. In Java, there is a class for every array type, so there's a class for int[] and similarly for float, double, etc. The direct superclass of an array type is Object. Every array type implements the interfaces Cloneable and java. In Java programming language, arrays are objects which are dynamically created and may be assigned to variables of type Object. All methods of class Object may be invoked on an array.

Output:

```
javac array_output.java
java array_output
i i i i i i i i i i
```

Hence, the correct option is (D).

16. Object initialization using new keyword involves constructor call whereas malloc does not involve constructor call. That's why new is explicitly added in C++. Also, malloc is used to assign memory to any pointer so it assigns memory equals to the size of the class however new keyword involves initialization also so calls the constructor of that class.

Hence, the correct option is (C).

17. Virtual inheritance is a C++ technique with which it ensures that a derived class contains only one copy of the base class's variables. In C++, it might mean private inheritance or virtual inheritance. Virtual inheritance is a C++ technique that ensures that only one copy of a base class's member variables are inherited by second-level derivatives. This feature is most useful for multiple inheritance, as it makes the virtual base a common subobject for the deriving class and all classes that are derived from it. This can be used to avoid the diamond problem.

Hence, the correct option is (A).

18. Delete is used to delete a single object initiated using new keyword whereas delete[] is used to delete a group of objects initiated with the new operator. The delete operator deallocates memory and calls the destructor for a single object created with new. The delete[] operator deallocates memory and calls destructors for an array of objects created with new[]. Delete is an operator that is used to destroy array and non-array (pointer) objects which are created by new expressions. The delete can be used by either using delete operator or delete[] operator.

Hence, the correct option is (C).

19. Do-while is called exit controlled loop because in do-while termination condition is checked when we have executed the body of the loop i.e. we are exiting the body and then checking the condition, therefore, it is called exit controlled loop. An exit control loop checks the condition for exit and if given condition for exit evaluates to true, control will exit from the loop body else control will enter again into the loop. Such type of loop controls the exit of the loop that's why it is called an exit control loop.

Hence, the correct option is (C).

20. Both while and for loops are called an entry-controlled loop because in both of them the termination condition is checked before we enter the body of the loop so, they are called an entry-controlled loop. An entry-controlled loop checks the condition at the time of entry. Only if the condition is true, the program control enters the body of the loop. Entry-controlled loops are used when checking of test condition is mandatory before executing loop body, whereas exit controlled is used when checking of test condition is mandatory after executing.

Hence, the correct option is (D).

21. Current position of the user is returned by watchPosition(). It update the position os th user as the user moves just like the GPS installed in a car. WatchPosition() method is stopped by clearWatch() method. For example: if(navigator.geolocation{navigator.watchPosition(showPosition);}

Hence, the correct option is (A).

22. Error callback function takes the oposition error object as its input parameter. The function is invoked by an unknown error occurred or if the user has denied sharing the information of the location or if the request timed out or if location information is unavailable. It does not happen when we are using wi-fi.

Hence, the correct option is (D).

23. The value of maximum age is positive long. Therefore, the maximum age returns time in milli-seconds. It specifies how long the user can use cached location data before using new location data. When its value is set to zero it indicates the user should not use cached location data and when set to zero is indicates the cached location data must be used by the user.

Hence, the correct option is (B).

24. The delay that occur during the playback of a stream is called Jitter. Jitter is when there is a time delay in the sending of these data packets over your network connection. This is often caused by network congestion, and sometimes route changes. Jitter can be the difference between a successful voice-over-internet protocol (VoIP) call and a disastrous, glitchy one.

Hence, the correct option is (C).

25. Algorithm that can be optimized to meet the timing deadlines and rate requirements of continuous media are Earliest-Deadline-First scheduling and SCAN-EDF scheduling.

The earliest deadline first (EDF) or least time to go is a dynamic priority scheduling algorithm used in real-time operating systems to place processes in a priority queue.

SCAN-EDF is a type of algorithm based on priority. SCAN-EDF serves non-periodic tasks only if there are no current real-time periodic tasks.

Hence, the correct option is (C).

26. External inputs, external outputs, external inquiries, internal logical files, external interface files are the five domains. A Function Point (FP) is a unit of measurement to express the amount of business functionality, an information system (as a product) provides to a user. FP measure software size. They are widely accepted as an industry standard for functional sizing. For sizing software based on FP, several recognized standards and/or public specifications have come into existence.

Hence, the correct option is (C).

27.

- A function point (FP) is a unit of measurement to express the amount of business functionality an information system provides to a user. FPs measure software size. They are widely accepted as an industry standard for functional sizing.
- Function Point Analysis (FPA) technique quantifies the functions contained within the software in terms that are meaningful to the software users. FPs consider the number of functions being developed based on the requirements specification.
- Function Points (FP) Counting is governed by a standard set of rules, processes and guidelines as defined by the International Function Point Users Group (IFPUG). These are published in Counting Practices Manual (CPM).

Hence, the correct option is (B).

28. MS-Access is a general-purpose database management system (DBMS) is a software system designed to allow the definition, creation, querying, update, and administration of databases. Well-known DBMS include MySQL, Microsoft SQL Server, Oracle, SAP, etc.

Hence, the correct option is (C).

29. Prism automatically replicates and moves data wherever it's needed across a vast network of computing facilities. In an intense big data-themed talk on Facebook's campus, the company revealed its latest infrastructure project. Codenamed

Prism, this project aims to solve one of the biggest problems Facebook has faced operating at its uniquely massive scale: How to create server clusters that can operate as a unit even when they're geographically distributed.

Hence, the correct option is (A).

30. If a combined function is used then it is the same form as the reduce function, except its output types are the intermediate key and value types (V2 and V3), so they can feed the reduce function. Streaming data includes a wide variety of data such as log files generated by customers using your mobile or web applications, e-commerce purchases, in-game player activity, information from social networks, financial trading floors, or geospatial services, and telemetry from connected devices or instrumentation in data.

Hence, the correct option is (D).

31. Document databases is a NoSQL Database Type. Document databases pair each key with a complex data structure known as a document. Document-oriented databases are one of the main categories of NoSQL databases, and the popularity of the term "document-oriented database" has grown with the use of the term NoSQL itself. XML databases are a subclass of document-oriented databases that are optimized to work with XML documents.

Hence, the correct option is (B).

32. Wide-column stores such as Cassandra and HBase are optimized for queries over large datasets, and store columns of data together, instead of rows. Cassandra is one of the most efficient and widely-used NoSQL databases. Another key benefit of Cassandra is the massive volume of data that the system can handle. It can effectively and efficiently handle huge amounts of data across multiple servers.

Hence, the correct option is (A).

33. Dynamic SQL is a programming technique that enables you to build SQL statements dynamically at runtime. You can create more general-purpose, flexible applications by using dynamic SQL because the full text of a SQL statement may be unknown at compilation. Embedded SQL, the SQL statements are identified at compile time using a preprocessor. The preprocessor submits the SQL statements to the database system for precompilation and optimization; then it replaces the SQL statements in the application program with appropriate code and function calls before invoking the programming-language compiler.

Hence, the correct option is (B).

34. The interface ResultSet has a method, getMetaData(), that returns a ResultSetMetaData object that contains metadata about the result set. ResultSetMetaData, in turn, has methods to find metadata information, such as the number of columns in the result, the name of a specified column, or the type of a specified column.

Hence, the correct option is (A).

35. \%ROWTYPE attribute is used for declaring a record variable that represents a full or partial row of a database table. The %ROWTYPE attribute provides a record type that represents a row in a database table. The record can store an entire row of data selected from the table or fetched from a cursor or cursor variable. Fields in a record and corresponding columns in a row have the same names and datatypes.

Hence, the correct option is (A).

36. Users use often terminal for access to mainframe or super computer. In the context of tele-communications, a terminal is a device that ends a tele-communications link and is the point at which a signal enters or leaves a network. Examples of terminal equipment include telephones, fax machines, computer terminals, printers and workstations.

Hence, the correct option is (A).

37. Data should be transmitted at the rate of 500 Mbps.

Transmission Time >= 2*Propagation Time

$$=> \frac{10000}{(500*1000000)} <= \frac{2*\text{length}}{200000}$$

=> lenght = 2 km (max)

Hence, the correct option is (B).

38. A parity bit, or check bit, is a bit added to a string of binary code. The parity bit ensures that the total number of 1-bits in the string is even or odd. Accordingly, there are two variants of parity bits: even parity bit and odd parity bit. In the case of even parity, for a given set of bits, the occurrences of bits whose value is 1 are counted. If that count is odd, the parity bit value is set to 1, making the total count of occurrences of 1s in the whole set (including the parity bit) an even number.

Hence, the correct option is (C).

39. A combination of hardware and software, which provides facilities sending and rationing of information between computer devices is called a Network. A network is a collection of computers, servers, mainframes, network devices, peripherals, or other devices connected to allow data sharing. An example of a network is the Internet, which connects millions of people all over the world.

Hence, the correct option is (A).

40. Server is a computer which provides resources to other computers commuted in a network. A server is a computer or system that provides resources, data, services, or programs to other computers, known as clients, over a network. In theory, whenever computers share resources with client machines they are considered servers.

Hence, the correct option is (A).

// Notes //

// Notes //

www.ingramcontent.com/pod-product-compliance
Ingram Content Group UK Ltd.
Pitfield, Milton Keynes, MK11 3LW, UK
UKHW061705190726
13853UKWH00008B/2406

9 789355 560315